D0883967

3 8077 1002 5414 7

Radical Alternative

Radical Alternative

STUDIES IN LIBERALISM BY THE
OXFORD LIBERAL GROUP

R. B. McCallum

Mark Bonham Carter

Peter Wiles · Walter Eltis

A. D. C. Peterson

Ian Bush · H. S. Deighton

EDITED BY

George Watson

1962

EYRE & SPOTTISWOODE

LONDON

COLLEGE OF THE SEQUOIAS
LIBRARY

First published 1962 by
Eyre & Spottiswoode (Publishers) Ltd
22 Henrietta Street, London WC2
© *1962 by the Oxford Liberal Group*
Printed in Great Britain by
Billing & Sons Ltd, Guildford, Surrey
Catalogue No 6/2492/1

Contents

To the memory of

NEVILLE WARD-PERKINS

1917-1960

economist, teacher, and founder of

the Oxford Liberal Group

whose generous exertions in his professional

and political interests are remembered

by his friends

Preface

The Oxford Liberal Group was founded in October 1959, immediately after the news of the Liberal advance in the General Election of that month. Among its first members were Neville Ward-Perkins, Lord Beveridge, Lord Franks (then Sir Oliver Franks), Mr R. B. McCallum, Professor Max Beloff, Mr Guy Wint, Mr A. D. C. Peterson, Mr W. Harford Thomas, Mrs Sylvia Chilver, Mrs Margaret Dawes, and a number of other Liberals in the Oxford region; and it took as its object the study and promotion of Liberal policies, and the encouragement of Liberal associations near Oxford. Since 1959 the Group has held discussions, offered help to neighbouring associations, and issued publications.

This is our first book. The portents of Liberal progress in Britain, so clear that neither enemies nor doubting friends can now deny them, are the fruits of hard work and optimism in which we have been glad to share. We thank the Liberal Party and the Unservile State Group, as well as many Oxford friends whose names are not recorded as contributors, for advice and encouragement in writing this book. Each chapter, however, represents the views of the author alone.

GEORGE WATSON

May 1962

Introduction

by

R. B. McCALLUM

It is the measure of Mr Jo Grimond's leadership of the Liberal Party that he has succeeded in providing an alternative, and that a radical one. We use the word *radical,* first of all, in its etymological sense of going to the roots of politics. A radical approach disregards makeshift expedients and the easy acceptance of institutions and practices which are too little examined, which survive through inertia of thought rather than by proven utility. There is need in our political thinking for what Professor Halévy has called 'intellectual virility'. It is radical, too, in the secondary and historical sense that it draws support from those traditions in English politics which have moved people to reflection, followed by ardent and continued demand for necessary change. We have had our Locke, our Adam Smith and our John Stuart Mill, and more recently Keynes and Beveridge. And we have had our leaders who in the practical world of government have grasped nettles, and carried through what was needed in the light of reason and justice against the forces of mere tradition and interests – the statesmen who carried the great Reform Bill, Cobden, Gladstone, Asquith, and Lloyd George. Various as the achievements and characters of these men were, they had this in common: that they were capable of full-swinging hard-going measures – the reform of the franchise, full free trade, the ending of the unlimited powers of the Lords, and the financial and social acts which laid the foundations of our social, but not socialist, democracy.

The signs that people in this country are looking for radical leadership are manifest in many ways. The interchanging rule of the two larger parties, which have for so long monopolized the parliamentary representation of the country without fully representing it, is no longer taken for granted. The confidence-trick whereby electors were beguiled into thinking that they had no choice save that between Dum and Dee is wearing thin: a voice has been heard remarking that the Emperor after all has no clothes. It is becoming realized that in an election there may be such a thing as consumers' choice.

The sentiments with which the public view the two major parties differ widely. The emotions people feel about continued Conservative government are unlike those which they felt towards

the Socialists in 1951. Labour was regarded with weariness and
irritation. But this is not the same as the satiety which people now
feel about Conservative measures and Conservative leaders. We
have perhaps been a little unjust to the Attlee Administration. It
had some real achievements to its credit. Disengagement from
India and Burma was complete and sincere in the true radical
spirit. There were none of the half-measures and conflicting policies
which were to be feared if this task had fallen to the Tories. The
forging of links with the countries that form the NATO alliance
was clear and sensible and carried out despite the disgust which
the fellow-travelling section of the party felt and expressed, that
section which the Labour Party can never fully shake off or control.
Attlee's firm action on the first day of the Korean War showed an
ability to meet an emergency which compares favourably with
the wild and catastrophic plunge of the Suez ultimatum. In
domestic affairs the Labour Government carried out some
measures of socialization which seemed politically necessary, the
socialization of the mines and the railways. If this was carried
further into electricity and gas, it is difficult to know whether we
are now better off than if these had been left to large-scale capitalist
enterprise. But the government fell into the characteristic errors
of doctrinaire socialism. It sustained a belief in cheap money when
the need of the economy demanded change. It had to devalue the
currency, and when the government was near its end it was faced
with a payments crisis so grave that it was fortunate not to survive
to deal with it.

But much of the displeasure of the electors with Labour was
not so much the result of its measures but with the cant by which
they were accompanied, and the illusions to which they held on
so pathetically after they had been scattered by the harsh winds of
reality. The simple faith in 'planning' sustained throughout the
war and after, the prim faith in the gentleman in Whitehall, were
a defiance of the common sense of the people. The drip-drip of
socialist jargon was becoming all the time more meaningless.
The occasional hiss of the class war and references to 'vermin'
shook the faith of ordinary men with the party which had
dedicated itself to the Brotherhood of Mankind. It caused
no deep fear: this rasping cry of the Jacobin who could command no tumbrils was ridiculous, no more. But it was con-
fidence-sapping in a high degree. Moreover, no sooner were the

socialized industries set up than it became plain that the assumptions so blandly made about them were ludicrously falsified. It had been said that if the changes were likely to be painful and difficult all would be set right by the alchemy of the socialist spirit. No one really knew beforehand whether, when the workers no longer toiled for the benefit of the few but of a socialized industry, they would work harder and better. We had been told that when no profit would any longer accrue to individual shareholders but to the whole community (in the old socialist prognostics not much was heard about loss) there would be an outpouring of energy, energy drawn from the strong arms and willing hearts of free men. But the difference was not perceptible. In a moment of time the old illusion vanished. We heard of lower production, of unofficial strikes, of demarcation-lines, and of other obstacles old and familiar. The new bureaucrats were no better than the old bosses. We had all speculated about the question whether public ownership would provide a new incentive. The answer was 'No'. Vesting day, the day on which each industry ceased to be a capitalist company and became a national board, proved to be no Pentecost. It was indeed a very minor festival.

Very different are our present rulers. Quietly in 1951 they climbed back into power. They made no apocalyptic claims. It sufficed that they were no longer the socialist schoolmasters. It is significant of the advance of democracy and of the milder political manners of our time that the word 'cad' was no longer heard. The Conservatives did not claim to be 'the masters now'. They thought they always had been and ought so to be. They were fortunate in being able to relax the austerities of the nineteen-forties, fortunate in being able to see the people enjoying the continued products of technical improvement. They have presided graciously enough over the distribution of naturally growing wealth, and in justice it must be said that their belief that capitalist enterprise would produce and distribute its material benefits has in part been fulfilled. The complaint against them has been their lack of imagination and action, of foresight and intelligent anticipation of needs and opportunities. It is not in the nature of conservative minds to make acute diagnoses which call for heroic measures or preventive medicine. Like a genial family doctor, deficient in scientific knowledge but sustained by a happy pragmatism, they have taken the optimistic view, relying on rest, sleep, and fresh air and the healing lapse of time to cure all ills. The occasional emetic of a high bank-rate and of credit squeeze has been the limit of their pharmaceutical treatment. Should the patient get worse, he can go to hospital.

So we have 'gone to hospital' over Egypt and Suez, we have gone to hospital over Cyprus, we are going to hospital over Central Africa. And on the most challenging and imaginative project of the time, the growth of a unifying, vital community in Western Europe, their approach has been the same. Foreign travel was deprecated; Sidmouth will suffice, until the long-term symptoms of the patient and his desperate need for sun and warmth brought the qualified verdict that going abroad may at last be tolerated. Modern Conservatives are fond of the verdict passed on the great whig statesman Walpole that he knew how to work 'within the limits of the possible'. This means, in Tory speech, what the Conservative leadership conceives at the time as the possible. The Treaty of Rome, the Common Market at the time of its inception, was not 'within the limits of the possible'. A hurried change is taking place in the fear that if we do not move the Common Market will be outside the limit of the possible, no longer a fruit outlandish and unripe, but a chance that may be ruinously lost.

In our relations with other powers in the world, with the rapid and dangerous movements in many parts of the globe, we must think no longer on traditional lines. We must estimate the lesser degree of power and importance which the British Government now enjoys and face it squarely without making gestures of total despair, an attitude popular with the troglodytes of the extreme left. This lesser degree of power and influence is two-fold. There is the reduced military and economic power of the United Kingdom; there is also the fact that the power which British electors direct and control is that of the United Kingdom only and not of any Empire or recognizable body of like-minded member-states of a Commonwealth which can be expected to act as a unit. These are things which the Conservative mind has been slow to recognize. The pathetic attempt of the Tories to try to trail faint clouds of glory from the vanishing tail of what had once been the bright comet of Empire might be excusable if it were not dangerous. And here Liberals may claim to have something in their intellectual inheritance natural to those who have sat at the feet of

Adam Smith or Mill, and superior to those who have formed their ideas from the sentimental and quasi-magical illusions of Disraeli. Politics has its logic which rejects the opium dreams of a vanished past. Not that we should be blind to what is real and durable in the Commonwealth connection. The young Liberals, especially, are more likely to be realistic and unprejudiced about this.

The rivalry of America and Russia dominates world politics now. But the situation changes, what seemed at one time to be the unassailable supremacy of the United States has been changed. What seemed to be the unbroken front of communist Russia and China is no longer secure. And in Europe the western lands, so rich and strong in wealth and talent, no longer appear as a mere no man's land in a struggle of titans. They are powerful, they move together with an ease that to those who remember the inter-war years seems almost miraculous. The Americans have favoured and fostered this. A great federation of states like the United States understands and favours federation. It is Britain, which might have led in this, that has lagged, partly because of narrow nationalist pride and nationalistic ignorance, and partly because of the fact that Britain has been what F. W. Maitland called 'a unicellular state'. Just as we could not, until forced to, contemplate a division of power between Westminster and Dublin, so we could not conceive a sharing of power with units of comparable power to ourselves. Here there would seem to be some real poverty of thought. Liberals may claim that the greatest of all our leaders, Gladstone, had the hardihood to see and to demand that we should be willing both to divide and to unite. A parliament in Dublin did not frighten or disgust him; the idea of a concert of Europe, an assembly of nations sharing responsibility for peace and progress, was always in his mind. For this reason more than any other he was hated almost to the point of mania by the Tories of his day. Such power to stand beyond the promptings of national pride was to them unnatural and abhorrent. This spirit is with us still. The small UNEF force sent to the Arab-Israeli border was greeted by Tory derision, but it is there still. If the United Nations forces, in their hard-pressed work in the Congo, should seem to stumble in their task, should take actions contrary to our prejudice, detraction descends upon them without measure. We are told that the younger generation will have little patience

with memories of Gladstone which their elders delight to invoke.
But a generation may find that while to them Gladstone is not
even a memory, he is something better – a discovery, the man
whose prophetic genius saw the errors of narrow political
pride, wrong in morals, wretched in practice, whatever the
cause for which it might be invoked, whether nation, empire,
or race.

If we turn our gaze from world problems to the domestic scene,
we may observe that there is one subject on which there is universal interest, and that is education. The young married couples
who have the final decision of an election in their hands have
many preoccupations. They may be irritated by a pay pause and
by grievances of a sectional kind which, within limits, they are
right to ventilate. But it is doing them a great injustice to suppose
that this is their only concern and that easier terms for their
mortgages, tax concessions on houses and income, will satisfy
their political malaise. This is the most vulgar of all social and
political errors. It is projected by one class upon another, by one
generation on another. It takes the form of remarking that 'all
they think about is' some boon or easement in the material conditions of their life. It is especially useful to take this line after
unfortunate experience in by-elections. It enables you to despise
the elements which have defeated you, and provides the welcome
hope that by some ingenious adjustments of policy or by favouring
winds of economic climate the shallow, foolish fellows and their
still more shallow, foolish wives will regain a proper sense of
where their bread is buttered. But these insulting suppositions
will recoil on those who hope to profit by them. It is not easy to
understand why it should be supposed that the sons and daughters,
the younger brothers and sisters of those who endured the blitz,
fought in countless battles in three continents, endured the perils
of keeping open the seas, should be deemed so little capable of
regarding anything but their immediate material interests. Interests
of course they have. The strongest is perhaps their interest in the
education of their children. It is probable that the great majority
of the younger parents today believe that they might have
enjoyed a better education than was actually given to them, and
they want above all to secure a better education for their young.
And this is not just a determination to scramble and fight, to save
and plan for their children alone. It is obvious to all who are

experienced in the educational profession today that this generation have a strong ethical and political sense about it. They conceive of it as a prime good for their own children, for others, and for the welfare of the whole society. The choice between using the state system or paying for the private system is a moral dilemma. To the merely democratically minded the state system may seem to be indicated. But to the liberal and individually minded there is the problem of the coils of an all-embracing state system with its threat to diversity of experiment, religious freedom, and personal liberty. These are grave matters on which people anxiously seek guidance.

Efficiency in education requires a great degree of specialization between children of varying talents. This is provided by the educational bureaucracy in the mechanism of the famous eleven-plus test. What are we to think about this? It has succeeded in providing a grammar school population from which to draw our more literate students and workers. But it divides society like a knife. Liberal philosophy views this with dismay. They seek a way out of this often cruel segregation. Those who can afford it may send their children to fee-paying independent schools where they will have similar educational opportunities and not be unfraternally separated. But even then the public schools, so-called, are working something similar in their joint entrance examination, which grows always stiffer, and new and more experimental schools are growing to supply the need. But should not parents who can afford fees do better to experience the state system and see with an experienced professional eye where it is needing improvement? Liberal educationists have something to say on this. But to the question 'what school should my child go to?' there is added another: 'what should he study when he is there?' This is perhaps even a more difficult question than the first. And the English educational system on examination appears to be in a too immobile state. More young people want to study the natural sciences and more are studying them, but the balance between one science and another, still more notably the balance between one modern language and another, is arbitrary and out of date. And strange to say it is no one's business to decide on these matters. We need to think hard about the institutional structure of our educational system. We know that there are education authorities. An Act of 1902 passed by the Conservative administration of Balfour provided this. Each county borough authority, London excepted, was the unit of education. If the councillors had not been elected with education in view, this was provided by a body of co-opted members of educational experience. And there the system still is, small local boroughs of under 100,000, large cities of nearly a million, small counties and large. They work hard, they are served by skilled and devoted education officers. But when all is said and done, one sees the authority, one is left to wonder about the education. They provide schools, they employ teachers; but neither they, nor the Ministry of Education, nor any other body, can give English education a strong impulsion to move with the times, to provide what is needed and desired. Here is a matter of prime importance. The question could be applied to the whole sphere of local government; but it is enough to ask whether these baronial castles, the education authorities, hurriedly built up by Balfour in 1902, are indeed the only or the best means of controlling our system. It may be that in central direction and not in local stagnation we will find the way of progress and adaptability in education.

While in arts the chief problem is the better teaching of foreign languages and the choice of which languages we need most to learn, there is need for more discrimination in the teaching of the natural sciences. Atomic power and the exploration of space has pushed physics far into the forefront. General enthusiasm for physics is everywhere apparent, but the direction of science studies as a whole requires a consideration that it does not yet receive. In this respect Liberals, while always viewing with caution too great a concentration of state power, will regard the treatment of science as a more or less unexplored field requiring the most earnest care. Within the sciences it seems that the physical sciences have run ahead in numbers and expenditure beyond the biological sciences. The present and possible developments in biological science, less known than in physics, open out prospects both encouraging and alarming which will require the attention of government and raise moral and even religious problems of great difficulty. For this reason it is all the more important that the public should know what is afoot and that the organization of science studies should be balanced and carefully directed. The problem here from the political side is difficult and subtle. Scientific discovery is conducted by many organizations, universities, learned societies, government departments and even industrial firms. Vast amounts of public money are spent. Yet the responsibility for science has been for long a general responsibility of the Lord President of the Council. The present President, Lord Hailsham, is certainly a person of distinction and he has been accorded the designation of Minister for Science. Yet his ministry is inadequately staffed and insufficiently centralized; he presides rather than directs. Do we know that this somewhat amateur method of coordinating scientific discoveries and resources is the best way? Is it indeed at all probable that it is the best?

And consideration of science takes us back to the mystery of Russian power. Curiosity about Russia is intense; travel there somewhat more frequent, but still only a trickle. Neglect of the teaching of Russian can only be described as calamitous. From the Liberal point of view the Russian state is the example of state tyranny over the individual. No degree of success in the material realm which it may attain will justify it to us. Yet there may be much to be learned from it. It has usually been felt here that we have on the one hand a civilization inherently superior because of its freedom and at the same time by our freedom and individuality bound in the long run to be superior in the material realm also. This attitude of 'all this and Heaven too', reminiscent of the atmosphere of the 1959 election, is dangerous. The ruthless direction of the Russian economy has advantages, especially in the compulsory saving of capital which it can impose upon its helpless citizens. Here we have drawbacks and handicaps: not fatal perhaps, not ruinous, but carefully to be measured and understood. And may it not be that even in their drab state-ridden culture they may have some merits and be free from some evils which we shrink from facing here? It is not by uncritical condemnations, by the launching of full-blooded ideological anathemas, that we can measure the dimensions of this great problem. Liberals will want to know more, to understand more clearly the truth about this civilization which is in so many ways the antithesis of our own; and while we must dare to reject much, we must also dare to recognize merits which may be too easily ignored and explained away.

In all these matters and many more, the authors of the essays in this book have tried to come to grips with some of the most vexing of current problems. Their title to be heard is their proficiency in their own profession, and what they have to say, whether palatable to other Liberals or not, arises from continuous and deep reflection. In this Introduction we can do no more than commend them to the respectful attention of readers willing to engage in patient and serious reflection on public affairs.

PART ONE

Liberals and the Political Future

MARK BONHAM CARTER

Since 1931, with a single interval of six years, this country has been governed by a Conservative, or Conservative dominated, administration. This is hardly an encouraging thought for anyone who is not a Conservative, and doubtless there are some Conservatives who would agree that a little real opposition, a spell on the opposition benches, a few years out of office for some ministers, would be no bad thing for their country or their party. But during the past generation this is how the 'two-party' system, of which we hear so much, has worked. It has led to what is virtually one-party government.

Moreover, for the British system to work efficiently, there is need for something more than a lively and active opposition. There must exist a credible alternative government which can step in and take over the administration at any moment. By a credible alternative I mean a body of men, backed by a policy which is known to their supporters and accepted by them. Judged by these standards the Labour Party does not represent such an alternative. It is not a credible but an incredible alternative.

The most important task in domestic politics over the next few years is to create such an alternative, to create an instrument able and willing to carry out radical policies. The Liberal Party is the nucleus round which such a party can gather.

But, it is commonly objected, there is no need for another 'Liberal Party'. The Conservative Party under the aegis of Mr Butler, Mr Macmillan and Mr Macleod has been liberalized and the backwoodsmen brought under control. Suez, like Munich before it, was an error which can now be forgotten, and the Conservative Party of today is not only liberal but contains within its ranks individuals who are proud to call themselves radicals. Even in Africa things have changed radically since Mr Macmillan, that canny judge of the political weather, noticed that a full gale was blowing – which it had been for a number of years. The wind of change speech, it is argued, was, after all, a great liberal statement.

But was it? Let us examine the wind of change speech as an example of Tory liberalism. Certainly it was greeted by the Tory press as an audacious speech, and as yet another example of the

Prime Minister's aptitude for stealing other people's clothes. It was also treated as liberal by others who should have known better. Yet, in fact, this could not be further from the truth. An examination of Mr Macmillan's words on that occasion will show that his speech, far from being a great Gladstonian statement of faith, imbued with liberal principles, was in fact a classic exposition of the Conservative position. Mr Macmillan drew the attention of his audience to a change in the weather that had already occurred and advised them to take the necessary precautions. He pointed out that their environment had altered and that, therefore, their policies must alter. It was as though he said, 'There is a gale blowing; if you want to keep warm, put on your coats.' He reported on a fact that he had observed, namely that:

> . . . the wind of change is blowing through the continent. The growth of national consciousness in Africa is a political fact and we must accept it as such.

The kernel of his message was that in existing circumstances the policy of the South African Government would not work.

The radical approach is precisely the opposite of this. What impresses the radical is not so much that *apartheid* does not work but that it should not work, and it is his purpose to create a society in which it cannot work.

One difference, therefore, between Left and Right, Liberal and Tory, Radical and Conservative – and I use these labels for want of any better – is this: the Left tries consciously to shape its own environment; the Right makes terms with the environment that surrounds it. The Left tries to impose a pattern upon nature; the Right accepts it as it is.

I am not saying that the position of the Right is indefensible. Far from it – it is a position which some people have always held, and it has a long and distinguished history in the development of political ideas. All I am concerned to point out is that there is a clear distinction between these two attitudes, and that no good purpose is served by pretending that the distinction does not exist or that the two really amount to the same thing.

Another example of the same attitude is expressed by Mr C. M. Woodhouse, Conservative Member for Oxford, in his *British Foreign Policy since the Second World War* (1961). There he

describes the world situation in which this country found itself
in 1959, in the following terms:

> For Britain in particular the outlook was encouraging; for
> Britain was not a power that wished to bring about radical
> changes in the world but to live with the world as it was (p. 244).

Those words might well have been spoken by the courtiers of
Canute or by Sir Samuel Hoare in the spring of 1939, and they
epitomize the fatal self-satisfaction which overcomes the British
Conservative Party when it has been in power too long. Consider
the assumptions Mr Woodhouse has made: that the world in
1959 was not in need of radical changes; that radical changes
would be to the disadvantage of Great Britain; that the outlook
was encouraging because it indicated that such radical changes
were unlikely in the foreseeable future – this written in an age of
scientific, economic and political revolution, in which the rate of
change is more rapid than ever before, its scope all-embracing and
its impact world-wide.

There is a further difference between radicalism and conservatism. The word 'radical', according to the Oxford English
Dictionary, means 'of or pertaining to root or roots'. In politics,
this word implies a belief that certain problems can only be tackled
by attacking them at their roots. To combine this belief with
Conservatism is to run clean contrary to one of the main streams
of conservative thought. Classic conservative thinking in this
country has been much concerned with society as a natural growth,
and the most important part of this mythical plant is its roots. If
the plant is to survive, let alone to grow, its roots must at all
costs be preserved. Such, broadly speaking, is the message of
Burke's *Reflections on the Revolution in France* (1790):

> Upon that body and stock of inheritance, we have taken care
> not to inoculate any scion alien to the nature of the original
> plant.

From this analogy between society and a living organism all
sorts of misleading conclusions are derived. Society is said to
grow like a plant – steadily and regularly – and history is seen as
a continuous process of growth and decay.

A radical cannot see history, or for that matter society, in that
light. Events do not flow with the smooth progress of a placid

English stream interrupted by an occasional eddy. They sometimes arrive in batches, and the stream they resemble is a stream of cars which from time to time pile up one behind the other, making a traffic block, thus producing a new situation requiring radical action.

The very nature of events creates problems which demand radical solutions, and our own history is littered with examples of this all-too-familiar process. The series of technical innovations which constituted the Industrial Revolution did not occur at nicely spaced intervals, and its results engulfed society with all the force and all the surprise of an avalanche. The relations between the United Kingdom and Ireland are another example, and the settlement with India at the end of the last war was an example of a radical solution which could never have been carried through by a Conservative government.

The advent of nuclear power and its effect upon the art of war is yet another instance. Lord Alanbrooke reports a conversation with Sir Winston Churchill when news of the successful explosion of the first atomic device had just arrived. As he himself admits, Sir Winston's 'appreciation of its value in the future international balance was far more accurate than mine'. Sir Winston immediately appreciated that the advent of nuclear power was one of these events which has radical consequences. Lord Alanbrooke, with soldierly conservatism, did not. 'I tried to crush his over-optimism, based on the result of one experiment, and was asked with contempt what reason I had for minimizing the results of these discoveries. I was trying to dispel his dreams and as usual he did not like it.'[1]

But if this distinction is accepted, why (it may well be asked) should not the Labour Party be the representative of radicalism in this country? Here is a party with a great history, with notable achievements to its credit, backed by the massive machinery and financial power of the trade unions, and with a considerable representation in the House of Commons. Here, it might seem, are the people to whom we should turn as the alternative to the Conservatives.

Their recent record is, of course, the first answer to this question; but that in its turn requires explanation. The Labour Party suffers from a number of built-in disadvantages which

[1] Lord Alanbrooke, *Triumph in the West* (1959), p. 478.

prevent it from becoming the alternative we require in the second half of the twentieth century. First, it is historically a socialist party. This albatross still hangs round its neck, scaring away voters and forcing the leaders of the party to spend their time defending ideas in which they no longer believe instead of pursuing radical objectives of urgent importance. A Socialist Party is committed to altering the whole shape of society, a task beyond the very limited scope of parties and politicians. A Radical attacks certain critical aspects of existing society, thereby altering its nature at one remove.

Secondly, the Labour Party is committed to the idea of the working class as a solid and identifiable unit in the body politic. This is a wasting asset. In the future the homogeneity of the working class will soon have as little application in this country as it does in the United States of America. Moreover, the Labour Party must, with one half of its mind, actively desire the working class to remain homogeneous and proletarian – for this, after all, is the source of its strength. Yet this is hardly a progressive point of view. It leads unions to concentrate on the wrong objectives: to prefer workers to be wage earners rather than property owners; to neglect the task of breaking down the barriers which separate staff from shop floor; to pour cold water on schemes which encourage participation and which could help to destroy the distinctions between the various grades in industry.

Thirdly, the Labour Party is hobbled by its connection with the trade union movement, the source of its finance and among the most conservative forces in the country. The trade union movement is a producer movement and an established movement, now dominated by traditions which it collected in its ascent to power. The trade unions themselves should be the object of radical reform. Contracting in should be substituted for contracting out; their officers should be elected by secret ballot; the Registrar of Friendly Societies should be given more power to supervise the operation of their constitutions. Lastly, it is surely intolerable that owing to the block-vote system the political whims of a single trade union or of the leader of a trade union should have such a powerful influence on the policy of a major party. When you put these questions to a leading trade unionist, the defence presented is the pure milk of conservatism and, presumably, drawn from Burke.

There are other factors which prevent the Labour Party from being the radical alternative which the situation demands. Not least among these are the nature of its successes and the circumstances in which it achieved them between 1945 and 1951. There are many wise Conservatives today who thank their lucky stars they lost the General Election in 1945, though there is no evidence that the leaders of the party held this opinion at the time. Nonetheless, on looking back, it is obvious that during the last war, while one half of the nation's mind was concentrated on survival, the other half was looking forward to the fruits of victory; and as each year of war passed, so the expectations of what peace would bring became at once richer and less realistic. A nation at war is a nation suffering from an illness that may prove fatal. To survive, all its energies have to be mobilized and its will to live sustained. In the last war, our will to live was sustained by the hope of retaining after victory a status equal to that which we had enjoyed before the war, together with a degree of affluence that the sacrifices of the war made in the short run impossible. In a like manner a sick man, while he is in hospital, compares his recuperation to a holiday. It is only when he is failing to enjoy the irritations, frustrations, and the exhaustion which accompany recuperation that he almost longs to go back to hospital rather than return to the active business of ordinary life. It was the Labour Party's misfortune to be in office during the most painful years of this country's recuperation from the war, and many people look back on those years with all the distaste which they feel for the watering place they visited after a severe operation, the hotel they stayed in, the people they met, and the régime they followed at that time.

But if the period when it held office created in the public mind a series of associations between the Labour Party and those grey, disappointing years, so too the Labour Party developed during the same period habits of thought and emotional attitudes which it has been unable or unwilling to abandon. Nationalization, for instance, is an idea which has played an altogether exaggerated part in British politics since the war; and though Tory propaganda can take some credit for this, the conservatism of political thought in the Labour Party, its inflexibility, and the way in which it has allowed itself to be put on the defensive, is chiefly responsible. It is extraordinary that the British public should still regard nationalization as the major disaster of post-war policy when, after eleven years of Tory government, only road transport and a proportion of the steel industry has been denationalized, and when those aspects of nationalization which are most open to criticism – the structure of the nationalized corporation, and the absence both of parliamentary control and worker participation – have in all essentials remained unchanged. But there is little doubt that the majority of the electorate regards nationalization as 'bad' and that a succession of Conservative victories have been based on this single fact. Today Socialism is disliked because it is associated with nationalization on the Morrison model, not the other way round. What is amazing is that the Labour Party has simply accepted this situation. Recently, in the debate on Clause Four, it attempted to dissociate itself from this policy altogether. That it failed is hardly surprising. For the Labour Party to disown Socialism was perhaps expecting too much, but there was no reason why it should not have made greater efforts to explore new forms of public control, or why it should have adopted a position in which any suggestion that the Morrisonian corporation could be improved was treated as an attack upon itself, thereby projecting an image of itself inflexibly conservative and unwilling to learn from experience. The achievement of the Tory Party stands out in brilliant contrast: it has depicted itself as the great anti-nationalization party, in spite of having done little to alter it, taking credit at the same time for having left untouched the welfare schemes which Labour introduced and which the Tories in a dozen years failed to develop or refine.

The rigidity of the Labour Party's position on nationalization applies also to its attitude to other more important issues. While the Labour Party is still trying to disentangle itself from attitudes developed before 1951, the Tories forgot Munich within a few years, and Suez within two – their rate of repression keeping pace with that of technological change in the twentieth century.

The Labour Government made three major decisions affecting this country's external relations during its years of office. It invented the multi-racial Commonwealth; it repelled with incredulity the first approaches of the incipient European community; and it embarked on the process of making Britain an 'independent' nuclear power. All three have had serious and perhaps fatal consequences on the Labour Party's prospects of becoming a radical alternative to the Tories. A genuine hatred of imperialism inspired the first, and provided Lord Attlee with the ruthlessness that was necessary to grant India, Pakistan, and Ceylon their independence. But having by this one act abandoned the heartland of British imperial power, the Labour Party then found itself enthralled by a new mythology, and afflicted by what a distinguished Indian has described as 'a Commonwealth fixation'. Composed of the old dominions and the newly independent republics, this new multi-racial Utopia was to be held together by sentiment and 'governed' by influence. Britain would stand at its centre, though at the centre of what it would be difficult to define; for if one thing was certain it was that the members of the Commonwealth wanted independence and that the idea of developing a political or military or economic community was precisely that which they thought they had successfully escaped.

Stimulated by this rather loose ideal, and preoccupied with the problems of constructing a democratic Socialist society in post-war England, the Labour Party looked on the radical experiments which were developing in Europe and which were being pushed forward there by non-Socialist parties with all the jaundiced scepticism of the Football Association towards European teams.

As for the decision to make Britain an independent nuclear power, this was in the course of time to expose the Achilles heel of the Labour movement.

After six years of office, then, the Labour Party found itself landed with a thoroughly unpopular domestic policy and in foreign affairs burdened with a number of attitudes which could never be realized in practice. That it failed to recognize the sterility of its position more quickly in the face of a succession of electoral defeats is partly due to the structure of the party itself, and partly to the meagre quality of its intellectual inheritance. The last may seem a strange charge to bring against a party which is generally accused of being dominated by intellectuals. But intellectuals can be as unoriginal as the rest of humanity, and the leading Socialist thinkers of the 1920s and 1930s added singularly little that was new to political thought. Cole and Laski were expositors of other people's ideas; they translated a vigorous nineteenth-century doctrine into an emasculated form which they thought (wrongly) suitable to the British political climate; they were hardly pioneers; they were rather teachers who made converts among their pupils.

The most important contribution to the political thought of that period came from a Liberal economist, Maynard Keynes, and the adoption of his ideas helped, as he knew it would, those who wished to develop some kind of managed free enterprise and undermined the position of those to whom capitalism and the profit motive in any form were anathema. Similarly, the most influential academic practitioner in the political field, Lord Beveridge, was also a Liberal who, by extending the scope and efficiency of the welfare schemes inaugurated by the Liberal Government of 1906, helped to protect the individual from the harsher consequences of capitalism and lowered the social and political temperature of the times.

The poverty, the unoriginal and antediluvian quality of the Labour Party's intellectual inheritance, the memory of pre-Keynesian unemployment in the 1920s and 1930s, together with the disproportionate and conservative influence exerted by the trade unions within the Labour Party, and the Party's own record in office – all were factors which helped to prevent the largest progressive party in this country from looking bravely at our new position. In this Labour reflected one aspect of the national mood. But its failure was that it did so unconsciously, indeed sincerely, unaware that it was the task of a radical party in these years to face the realities of the twentieth century and to lead the way to new policies and new opportunities. Perhaps this universal complacency was part of the price we had to pay for victory. In Western Europe, where every country had been defeated and occupied in the course of six years of war by some other country, the end of the war was the beginning of a period of national re-appraisal. Not one of the great continental states of Western Europe could pretend that it had emerged from the war with much glory, or that the history of the previous two decades had vindicated either its leaders or its political system. Either defeat had been succeeded by liberation at the hands of others, or, as in Germany, a victory had been won so ghastly in its implications that even the horrors and humiliations of total surrender could never wipe away the haunting memory. Any government which gained power after those nightmare years was bound to be radical, in the sense that the roots of Europe had been laid bare. A fresh start was not a voluntary choice, it was the only possibility. And given the eternal vitality of the peoples of Western Europe, that new ideas and new policies should develop was at least predictable if not, as nothing is in politics, inevitable. The governments may have been Christian Democrat in complexion, but this did not prevent the Italian Government owning shares in private industry as a matter of course, or the social services in Germany being a charge on privately owned firms, or France developing a highly successful system of central planning. Indeed in France, the despised, distrusted and allegedly corrupt politicians of the Fourth Republic, who broke every rule of British party government (supposing they knew them), were the source of almost every idea that today makes Europe exciting.

Meanwhile in England we were remembering V.E. day, V.J. day, our victories in the Western Desert, the agony of Dunkirk, the Battle of Britain and, above all, the days when we stood alone. To stand alone was never a policy advocated by a responsible British statesman until Goschen, in a moment of hubris or myopia, uttered something about splendid isolation. The whole policy of *perfide Albion* has been an attempt to avoid this lonely and desperate condition. If in war to stand alone may on occasion be a disagreeable necessity, in peace it is no policy at all. Nor is it a fair description of British policy since 1945. It would be more accurate to say that the United Kingdom has failed adequately to appreciate the consequences of the allied victory in 1945 and that as a result, while fostering to an exaggerated degree our special position with the USA, we developed an attitude that was inward-looking rather than outward-looking. For this the Labour Party must bear even more responsibility than the Conservatives. Never has our position in Europe stood higher than in 1945. But the lead for which our continental neighbours were looking was not forthcoming from the government of this country.

It is of course true that everyone who came to maturity before 1939 saw the United Kingdom as a 'great power', that is as a power which could decide the issue of war and peace. Nor were they altogether mistaken, for after all we decided for peace in 1938 and for war in 1939, with all the consequences that those decisions carried. Yet on both occasions our ability to direct the course of events depended on a series of historical accidents. Even in that short period in the nineteenth century when our pre-eminence was virtually unquestioned, it arose from the defeat of Napoleon in 1815, the disunity of Germany, the fact that Russia remained a medieval kingdom and that America chose to develop her strength in private. In these circumstances, despite our small population and minuscule resources, we were able to act as a great power. It was a *tour de force* which continued to exercise an influence over men's minds when the balance of power had shifted against us. Even after 1918 the Americans liked to think that British supremacy still obtained, for it absolved them from responsibility, the Russians were engaged in an absorbing political experiment, the French were exhausted, and the Nazis planning a particularly horrible revenge on the rest of the world. It was somewhat in this fashion that the illusion of British power persisted through the 1920s and 1930s despite innumerable indications that the substance was no longer there.

In any case, no one resigns from the position of top dog immediately after a famous victory, and there were plenty of reasons for the British retaining their illusions of grandeur after 1945 – not least the fact that their leaders had all been brought up on history books written by men of the nineteenth century. For Mr Churchill, Mr Attlee, Mr Eden, and Mr Macmillan the greatness of Great Britain was something that had to be disproved before the facts could be allowed to speak for themselves, and the reappraisal of our role in the twentieth century made. Sir Winston, I cannot but feel, understood what had happened and it was this that led him to launch the European movement in 1947. It was only after he had regained office in 1951 that the years began to tell and pressure from the Conservative Party – to which he was, for once, under an obligation – was able to work effectively against his political instincts. If only he had been ten years younger, how different things could have been! Sir Anthony Eden might well have found his talents better used in working out a European policy already laid down rather than swimming about in search of a role which he so disastrously chose for himself and his country.

Yet the fact remains that from 1945 onwards this country has been inward-looking – not only in its foreign policy but also in most of its other activities. It has been a period, perhaps like the Restoration, during which, after great exertions, the British people have rested on their oars and, latterly, thought they were enjoying themselves. While they have watched the excesses of contemporary society proliferate in an era of moral and intellectual indolence, we must hope they have been re-charging their batteries

and gathering their energies for a new effort which we will see in
the next decade. But if we exclude the memorable achievements of
the Labour Government in the field of social welfare, the years
of concealed adjustment have little enough to show for themselves, and what they have shown is mainly negative. We did not
have an Algeria, a McCarthy, nor (despite Lord Beaverbrook) did
we make a last humiliating attempt to build an imperial bloc.
Nevertheless, we have had to pay for our refusal to look in the
mirror and see ourselves as we are. British policy since the war
has been marked by a series of attempts to do more than we could,
to influence events where our power to do so has been unequal
to the task, and by a failure to exert the influence we possess in
those areas where it could have been used decisively.

It is the task of a radical party to make a re-appraisal of the
British position and having made it to lead the country in new
directions. There is nothing shameful in not being a great power,
nor is it necessarily boring. For the bulk of our history we have
had to make terms with our more powerful neighbours and
develop a way of life in conformity with our means. Since the
great powers of the twentieth century have little room to
manoeuvre, and since their posture is of necessity pretty rigid, an
escape from the world's predicament may well be found by those
who, having experienced greatness, have recently descended into
the middle ranks. They can afford to experiment with new types
of political association; indeed they must. It is for them to
develop forms of international co-operation, perhaps a pattern of
international democracy, which may allow the tiny world we share
with so many other societies at such contrasting levels of development to develop without the total destruction of us all, but which,
at the same time, will have to take into account the enduring fact
that, although some societies will always regard others as bad, to
treat them as intolerable is today to jeopardize the survival of
mankind.

It is not my task in this chapter to draw up a manifesto for a
radical party. But after many years of stagnant government,
Britain is littered with issues which demand radical treatment, and
in a society in which political loyalties appear to have become
more fluid it is worth trying to point the direction in which we
can move, if we so wish.

The United Kingdom is not yet an affluent society, but affluence is now attainable and, indeed, is something most devoutly to be desired and worked for. A damaging criticism of recent governments is that, despite the Conservatives having transformed themselves into a strictly materialist party, they have failed to lead this country towards affluence at the same pace or with the same determination as our neighbours and competitors. The means by which affluence can be attained is discussed elsewhere in this book, but the idea that it is, as such, an undesirable condition, and even faintly vulgar, is one that should be confuted and condemned. The main advantage of social affluence is a rather old-fashioned one. When a society attains a degree of wealth in which it is unnecessary for any of its members to live in poverty, the area of choice open to that society is greatly extended: decisions need not be dictated solely by economic criteria but can be made with other wider considerations in mind. Whole societies will find themselves in the position previously enjoyed only by privileged individuals and classes, and they will have the opportunity to choose – to choose between more material goods or more beauty, more work or more leisure, their immediate self-interest or their duty to the rest of the world. This situation will represent a revolution which will have to be reflected not only in our political thinking but also in our political institutions. To date, all societies have been governed in their policies by criteria which are either military or economic. The problem has been to survive attack by a hostile power and by a hostile environment. To gain control of one's environment made it likely that one would defeat a hostile power; to defeat a hostile power supposedly made it more likely that one would survive the assaults of a hostile environment. In the contemporary world the western (or northern) countries are in sight of controlling their physical environment to the extent that there is no danger of death from starvation, no real threat of poverty in the old sense, and there can exist a real bourgeois liberty on a scale that has never been contemplated in the past. Given the sensible use of the technology at our disposal, our streets can be paved with gold. The only thing which can destroy this prospect is the possibility of war and the fact that two-thirds of the world still live in a pre-affluent condition in which poverty is an ever-present fact and death by starvation, from plague, flood and famine, a day-to-day reality. Confronted by this inviting challenge, there are three main problems which we must solve:

(i) How to attain affluence as quickly as possible; and, in the process, how to build a civilized community;
(ii) How the affluent societies are to co-exist in peace with the rest of the world that still lives on the edge of starvation;
(iii) How to prevent the world from blowing itself up.

It is with certain limited aspects of the first of these problems that I am mainly concerned here. It is fairly obvious that the nation-state as we know it in Western Europe is inadequate as an economic instrument to make the most of the opportunities which modern technology offers. Encroachments on national sovereignty are necessary to ensure full employment, to control boom and slump, to provide sufficient currency reserves, to engage in space research – even to build a supersonic airliner. The record of the EEC is such as to lead one to suppose that, if and when we join it, it will have a stimulating affect on investment and expansion within this country. The possibilities of economic planning within a Europe which includes the United Kingdom are huge. The pooling of Western European currency reserves would allow this country to escape from a dilemma – either expansion or a strong pound, either stagnation or a run on sterling – which has crippled our economic progress since the war. Though the political arguments for integration are fundamental, the economic advantages cannot be neglected, unless one has no faith in British enterprise, skill or adaptability. Moreover, even the Labour Party was in favour of the original European Free Trade Area proposals for a purely economic association with Europe. Yet had they ever been put into practice, they would have led inevitably to an erosion of national sovereignty. Indeed by the end of the negotiations in 1958 this country was ready to agree to majority decisions on certain economic issues. With the exception of the lunatic fringe, therefore, hardly anyone would deny that, as far as economic progress is concerned, national sovereignty is an obstacle. We are living in an age when larger economic and political units are almost inevitable, and where those who refuse to combine because they wish to control their own destinies will find their fate decided without consultation, and generally to their disadvantage, by those who have joined.

But though in the twentieth century the advantages of size are such that we must accept them, many of the old arguments against bigness, and particularly against big political units, still have force. Indeed many of the troubles of contemporary government stem from the very size of the unit and from the difficulties of communication between government and the governed that follow from it. The sense of participation by the citizen in his own self-government that lies at the heart of democracy is lost. In addition, the complexity of contemporary government, the vast issues at stake, and the need for highly technical advice when it is added to the size of the units involved, has led to the concentration of more and more authority in the hands of individuals – de Gaulle, Adenauer, Kennedy – so that even in this country the Prime Minister's position has become quasi-presidential. It is only by concentrating the vast authority of the state in an individual, it is argued, that the ordinary citizen can feel that he is in touch with it – yet this is hardly a democratic trend, and the creation of political blocs like the EEC will obviously increase these problems. Certainly the absence of a sense of participation in the making of policy is at the root of many of our discontents today, not least among members of Parliament.

Few Members of Parliament would now claim that they are much more than the last court of appeal with the final power to dismiss the government. Few would deny that though they have some influence on policy-making, their influence is marginal compared with that of the great pressure groups like the civil service, the unions, the various organs of industry, and the City. Nor have they exercised this ultimate power for over twenty years, and even on that occasion, in the midst of the greatest crisis in the history of this country, in the summer of 1940, so atrophied were the muscles of the Mother of Parliaments that the government which resigned, resigned with a majority of eighty-one, only thirty-nine of its followers having screwed up the courage to vote against it.

Nor is the decline of parliamentary power surprising. The last major reform of our political machinery (apart from votes for women) was the Parliament Act of 1911, and this was the start of a job that was never completed. Since then much has happened – the world has survived two wars, we are living in the midst of a continuous scientific revolution, the structure and habits of society as a whole are being transformed, and the responsibilities of government have in all countries been greatly extended. Meanwhile Parliament has to all appearances remained unchanged, and those who have examined it have approached it with all the reverence of zoologists inspecting a coelacanth. Here, they seem to say, is a remarkable survival which still works. But does it? There is no example of British complacency more remarkable than our attitude to our parliamentary institutions and our unquestioning faith (for such it is) that they work. It is a faith that our ancestors never shared. Neither in the seventeenth century nor in the nineteenth century, both revolutionary ages like our own, were the English content to leave their parliamentary institutions as they found them. In both centuries they regarded what they found as totally inadequate for their purposes, and proceeded to change them in the most radical fashion, embarking on a series of adventurous experiments, defying convention, disregarding precedent, and producing as a result the basic machinery on which western democracy still rests. The seventeenth century saw a succession of parliamentary evolutions which were revolutionary in their effects, and the nineteenth century the extension of the franchise, the development of the party system as we know it (and worship it), culminating in the emasculation of the House of Lords.

Since when – nothing, except a steady decline in the power and prestige of Parliament and an equally steady increase in the amount of business which flows through the House of Commons. The most powerful men in the country no longer find it useful to sit in the House of Commons, and it is very doubtful if Parliament today provides an adequate reservoir of talent from which to form a government. Apart from Question Time, which, because it provides good copy for the Press, is a grossly overrated item in the parliamentary time-table, attendance in the Chamber is pitifully low, largely because MPs, who are underpaid and overworked, have ceased to be first and foremost our governors and have become instead a curious hybrid, area PROs for their respective parties and social welfare officers explaining the complex irrationality of contemporary government to their constituents.

Yet no one, as far as I know, apart from the Liberal Party, is interested in the reform of our governmental machine. The

Conservatives identify it with themselves; the Labour Party have never paid much attention to it, for inefficient and complex as it may be, compared to the constitution of the Labour Party it has all the rationality and simple beauty of Newtonian cosmology. Parliament needs another Bentham if it is not to become a road block in the way of radical reform. Alone among western democracies we retain an hereditary second chamber, and alone, to the best of my knowledge, we have refused to make use of specialized committees.

In the last sixty years the balance of power has moved inexorably in favour of the Minister and against the backbencher. The more complex legislation becomes and the wider the scope of the government's responsibility, the greater the disadvantages of the private member, who may well be without a room in which to work, or even a secretary to type his letters, and yet find himself in conflict with a Minister backed by the whole resources of the Civil Service. Though the annual ritual of the Finance Bill, taken on the floor of the House, provides a number of headlines about late-night sittings and maintains the fiction that the whole House is scrutinizing every penny of the Government's expenditure, it is a fiction, and a laborious and time-wasting fiction at that. The Committee Stage of all bills should be remitted to Standing Committees, and certainly the detailed examination of the nationalized industries should be the responsibility of specially appointed subordinate bodies. If the control exercised by shareholders over limited companies is slight, that of the House of Commons over the nationalized industries is no more stringent.

The argument in favour of specialized committees for, say, Defence or Foreign Affairs is equally strong. To acquire a reasonable knowledge of the fairly technical controversies on defence policy the citizen of this country has either to turn to the admirable reports of the Congressional Armed Services Committee of the United States or use the good offices of the Institute of Strategic Studies, which was also set up on an American initiative. It seems to me odd that the British should be unable to use techniques successfully employed in the USA and elsewhere to keep its elected representatives informed, and incredible to suppose that the participation of members of the House of Commons in the process of policy-making would not be improved if they were better informed. The setting up of specialized committees of the type of the Congressional Armed Services Committee, properly adapted to our needs, would be one step in the right direction. A second would be the development of bodies like Chatham House, the Institute of Strategic Studies, and the National Institute of Social and Economic Research, which would provide essential information for politicians, journalists, and other interested persons. The Civil Service is an admirable institution; it is also immensely and increasingly powerful. Good government depends on an effective opposition and an informed public, but the Opposition would be far more effective, the private member far better informed, if more bodies of the type I have mentioned were set up, preferably on British initiative, financed by British money, and deliberately developed into an effective counter-civil service.

But if the machinery of British Government is to be brought up to date, there are matters far more important to consider than the complex machinery of the House of Commons. We are saddled with an hereditary House of Lords, the existence of which is solemnly defended on grounds of line-breeding in livestock. Surely we should ask ourselves whether we want a second chamber at all, and if we do not, whether it would not be as well to abolish it. It is fairly clear that the majority of the Labour Party (and probably the majority of the House of Commons) do not believe in a bicameral legislature if the upper chamber is to be invested with any real power. In that case might it not be better to say so? and having said so, to get rid of this strange and inappropriate heritage from the past? Alternatively it is possible to believe in the utility of a second chamber, as I do. But in that case the second chamber must be reformed so that it can fulfil some of the functions which it can usefully perform. Yet this is precisely the kind of problem which the Conservative Party has never been prepared to face. The Parliament Act applied a tourniquet to one arm of the body politic and it has been withering ever since. By allowing a few life peers (appropriately named) to seep in, as a kind of blood transfusion, the process may be arrested, but not halted. Rather than a withered arm it is probably better to have no arm at all.

The House of Lords can be reformed in two totally different ways. The first way could be introduced quickly and easily and would bring considerable benefits. The second would entail a far more radical reorganization of the structure of government in this country. The first method involves simply the abolition of the hereditary element and the extension of the principle which led to the creation of life peers. The ablest and most powerful men in this country are no longer prepared to fight their way into the House of Commons, to spend long hours sitting on its benches or long week-ends currying the favour of the electorate. None the less, the government of this country would benefit from the services of these men. Neither Mr George Woodcock nor Mr Carron, neither the Chairmen of Shell nor of Unilever, have ever made an attempt to enter the House of Commons. It is significant that both Mr Bevin and Lord Woolton, two of the most important influences in creating the atmosphere of post-war political life, entered the Government as a result of the 1939 war. It is only necessary to compare the manner in which Mr Kennedy formed his administration in 1961 with that of Mr Macmillan in 1959 to be aware of the limitations imposed on a British Prime Minister. Mr Kennedy was able to scour the whole country for men (so is Mr Krushchev). He was not restricted to members of Congress. Big business, professional politicians, the universities, the TV networks, the Bar, the trade union movement – all were wells into which he could dip in order to create a ministry of all talents. Not so the Prime Minister of Great Britain, whose choice in 1959 was confined to the Conservative members of the House of Commons and the Conservative peers in the House of Lords (largely selected by line-breeding). If one were concerned simply with enlarging the reservoir of talent from which the administration could draw, the answer would be obvious. Abolish the hereditary principle, make the House of Lords an appointed body, fill it with individuals who could contribute to the good government of this country by their ability and experience, and leave it at that.

Yet such a solution would be a short-term answer to our problems. A second chamber of this sort would be no more than a sub-committee of the House of Commons and would be open to many obvious objections. It would not constitute a true upper house, it would be unable to provide any real check on the activities of the House of Commons, it would increase the patronage at the disposal of the majority party. An effective second chamber in the United Kingdom must envisage the possibility of conflict with the House of Commons. If it is thought that the two will always act in perfect harmony, there is everything to be said for only having one – the harmony will then be complete. It is only through conflict that the second chamber can perform its function as a brake and a stimulus. In the classical arguments for and against a bicameral legislature, the chief emphasis has generally been laid on the second chamber as a brake, but I suspect that this is largely because in the past second chambers have been constituted to represent and protect conservative interests. There is no reason why a second chamber should not be devised to promote progressive views – and if the record of the United States Senate is taken into account, there can be no doubt that, progressive or otherwise, the Senate has often taken a more enlightened view of the true interests of the United States than the House of Representatives. Certainly in foreign affairs it would be difficult to find in the House of Representatives figures such as Senator Vandenberg and Senator Fulbright, who used their large influence consciously to involve the United States in world affairs. Members of a second chamber, given reasonable security of tenure and elected on a reasonable franchise, can act with greater independence of their party than the contemporary member of the House of Commons in this country, and it would be a 'progressive' measure to introduce an element into the British constitution which checked the growing power of the contemporary party machine.

A House of Lords which set up committees with powers to examine the working of Government departments, and whose members had sufficient independence to discuss new ideas and new issues, would be able not only to take a heavy burden of work off the shoulders of the House of Commons, but could also act as a spur to efficiency and an agent of realism which this country sorely requires.

But if it is to perform any of these functions, and above all if it is to come into conflict with the House of Commons, a reformed House of Lords must possess some basis for its authority. It must believe that when conflict is joined it has some chance of winning. In the past the authority of the House of Lords was founded on heredity and the landed interest, principles which in this country happened to coincide, and which were accepted by the majority of the politically effective population. For centuries

most people believed that heredity provided sufficient grounds
for parliamentary representation, and so long as the economy was
largely agricultural there were excellent reasons for ensuring that
the landed interest had a special place in Parliament. The Industrial
Revolution changed all that, and the waning power of the House
of Lords was finally written into the Constitution in the Parliament
Act of 1911. Under that Act the House of Lords still retained
authority to delay non-fiscal legislation passed by the House of
Commons, though there are few major instances of its having
used this authority. Such self-restraint is typical of a vested interest
on the defensive, but after 1911, and even more after 1945, the
House of Lords was aware that it was not on the defensive. It was
defeated. To use its residual powers would have been to invite
extinction – better to survive in decorative impotence, the
cavaliere servente of the popular chamber – such was the role chosen
by the descendants of our feudal and post-feudal aristocracy.

In the Darwinian world of politics the impotent do not survive.
If it is to survive, the House of Lords must become effective and,
if it is to become effective, it must find some basis for its authority
other than the hereditary principle. Two alternatives have been
widely canvassed. The first generally involves some form of
indirect election. Either members of the upper chamber are
elected by members of the popular chamber or, alternatively, they
are elected on some different franchise. Systems of this type have
been tried out at various times and in various places, but never,
to my knowledge, have they produced an effective second chamber. In so far as democratic principles are accepted, the popular
chamber is bound in such circumstances to be the victor. If it is
agreed that the will of the people is the question at issue, there can
be no doubt as to who represents it most accurately. Under such
a system the upper chamber is treated simply as a pasture in which
old horses can be put out to graze and, bereft of the traditions
which even the House of Lords manages to retain in a ghostly
way, such a body is, if possible, still less effective.

Alternatively it has been proposed that the House of Lords
should represent economic interests; that trade unions and
industries should elect representatives, introducing a corporative
element into the British Constitution. Such a suggestion can be
dismissed out of hand. The United Kingdom has suffered for
many years from excessive economic rigidity, the heritage of

unemployment and conservatism; what it needs is greater flexibility. To create a second chamber which embodied existing economic interests would be to provide a political weapon for the established which they would use effectively to suppress new methods, new ideas – indeed change and progress in all directions. In any case established economic interests are all too powerful as things stand without providing them with additional means of frustrating enterprise.

There is, however, a third possibility, another principle, on which the House of Lords might be based, and because it would differ from that of the House of Commons, it would be a stronger foundation for its authority. The principle which I have in mind is that the Upper Chamber should represent geographical or regional units in this country, which is, of course, the principle from which the Senate in the United States, the only effective second chamber in the world, derives its power. The Senate was created to preserve the identity of sovereign states within a federation. The House of Lords which I propose should be constituted to provide variety within an over-centralized nation state. Although the form might be similar, the purpose of these two bodies would be diametrically opposite.

I have always felt considerable sympathy for Scottish and Welsh nationalists in spite of the fact that the bulk of what they say is nonsense, and reactionary nonsense at that. When they claim that the political and cultural life of this country is unduly centralized, that everything is (as the popular saying goes) run from Whitehall, that there is in the British Isles a progressive atrophy of provincial life and an aggressive metropolitan culture which is obliterating all variety, they are not only speaking the truth but are also expressing the feelings of large numbers of people, neither Scottish nor Welsh, but English, who live outside the immediate orbit of London and the home counties. The homogenization of British culture is something to be resisted. The variety of British provincial life is something to be preserved and fought for, and it can easily be represented in our political arrangements.

In addition to Scotland and Wales, Devon and Cornwall, Wessex, the Home Counties (and/or London), the Midlands centred on Birmingham, East Anglia, Yorkshire plus Durham and Northumberland, Lancashire and Cheshire plus Cumberland and Westmorland – these areas, with a number of variations, have a genuine geographical, historical and economic unity. They have interests and character in common. They could be represented. Moreover, it is noticeable that units of this size seem to be more relevant to modern needs than the old county, which emerged from a series of historical accidents. The gas, electricity, and hospital boards of today are based on regional, not county, units. Town-and-country planning is bound to follow a similar pattern – and, in the last war, the country was divided for a variety of purposes into regions of this order.

But, above all, the regional interest is one for which people have a very real and intelligible respect, which is not directly related to the population which inhabits the region in question. Lancashire means something which cannot be judged in terms of the number of Lancastrians there happen to be at any date. Devon and Cornwall is in many ways a more coherent geographical and economic unit than Wales, which has always been divided between north and south. The population of Devon and Cornwall is not very large, and as a consequence its interests can only be inadequately represented in the House of Commons. But members of an upper chamber, elected to represent Devon and Cornwall, would not only represent an area with a very real character and history of its own; they would also speak for two major industries, agriculture and tourism, and they would speak with great authority. Their authority would be increased if they were elected by some form of P.R. and for a fixed period of years.

A House of Lords elected on a regional principle, which recalls the scheme for a heptarchy proposed by Sir Winston Churchill before the first World War, would certainly develop into a second chamber with sufficient authority to take business out of the House of Commons and even to disagree with it – a prospect the House of Commons might well find unwelcome.

One reform leads to another. A radical change in the construction of Parliament should lead to an equally radical reform of our system of local government. Today democracy must resist undue centralization and encourage not only provincial vitality, but also the participation of the ordinary citizen in his own self-government. At present our system of local government is failing in both respects because, while some of its units are too big, its biggest units are certainly too small to fulfil their functions without undue financial dependence on the central government. Given a second chamber elected on a regional basis, the same regions could also become the largest units in a reformed system of local government. Their powers would be extended and, in particular, the rates should no longer be their sole source of revenue. If the regions were granted a reasonable measure of financial independence, they could also have real authority in the fields of health, education and, above all, town-and-country planning. They would be perfectly well equipped to undertake these responsibilities. Each would contain within its borders at least two universities (with the exception of Wales), and the very fact that the authority of local government had been greatly increased would encourage men of ability to engage in it. It would become an exciting and constructive challenge. Many MPs, sitting weary hours on the back benches of the House of Commons, would be only too delighted to undertake such a task, and the House of Commons, relieved of the responsibility of supervising too much inadequately, might be able to perform its true task of overseeing our national purposes more adequately.

Regions such as these would be able to escape the dead hand of Whitehall, to experiment with new methods which answer the needs of their particular locality, and to respond to the demands of those who live there. But devolution of this sort implies the acceptance of a very important corollary, which many contemporary socialists and conservatives (paternalists both) would be loath to admit. The regions must be allowed to manage their affairs badly.

The strongest objection to any scheme of this sort will come from the educationists – from schoolmasters and dons. They will throw up their hands in horror at the very thought of persuading the people to support their purposes. How much more comfortable it is, they argue, to deal with educated civil servants at the Ministry of Education than with the philistines on the County Education Committees.

This is a perfectly valid argument against democracy as a whole and against the participation of people in their own self-government. It is a strong argument in favour of government by an educated élite chosen by competitive examination rather than by the ballot box. But if an affluent democracy is to be civilized, then it must be truly self-governing, and we cannot deliberately create a society which is civilized only because its institutions are so arranged that in their working they are undemocratic.

A double reform of this sort, which altered the nature of our second chamber and re-defined the boundaries of our local government units, would provide a balance to set against the central proposal for international integration put forward in the first part of this chapter. The larger international units become, the more powerful the central organs which control them; and the greater the extent of national sovereignty which individual nations abandon, the more urgent is the need for internal devolution. If large units such as the EEC are to develop into real political entities with a common foreign policy, a common defence policy, and a genuine feeling of duty towards the outside world, it is vitally important to develop an effective political machinery which can balance the powerful contemporary forces for centralization, which will encourage variety and experiment and make popular participation in government a reality.

PART TWO

The Economy and the Cold War

PETER WILES

Year by year it becomes more probable that the Cold War has been lost. To an utterly ruthless dynamism stands opposed a half-unscrupulous stagnation. Small countries are undermined, bought, or genuinely converted, rates of economic growth diverge, pessimism and uncertainty spread.

And yet the future is eternally unpredictable, and history helps only those who go on trying, those who help themselves. It crushes those who cease to fight and hope. This chapter is devoted to what must be called the Cold War on the domestic front, especially the economic front: is our basic economic order really so terrible, how can we improve it, what is our ultimate vision of it? We impinge, of course, at many points on foreign affairs, but fundamentally the answer is always the same: whether we base foreign policy on aid or missiles or subversion or mere domestic example, we need a strong economy, fully employed, rapidly growing, able to generate a surplus, and socially just. We also need a less squalid society.

These things are of course wanted for their own sake, and very much that is here written would have been written had there been no Communism upon the face of the earth. Yet much also must be different because of it, and I make no apology for linking the domestic scene with the Cold War. I am old-fashioned enough to believe that we are in a competition with something thoroughly evil that will never relent and that will prove irreversible if it once wins; and new-fangled enough to want to try unorthodox and peaceful ways of beating it. What we are fighting for is not, of course, only wealth: Communism could give us that. It is human freedom and decency, humour and tolerance, elegance and idleness, the right to be absurd, eccentric and cussed. In a word, we are fighting for the individual as such; and this is relevant to the economic order, which is not there simply to produce wealth. Our main problem is precisely how much we must sacrifice the individual to economic growth now in order to meet the external threat to his very existence.

This exordium is best ended with a disclaimer. It is not illiberal to take Communism seriously. On the contrary, it is illiberal to play it down. Apocalyptic warnings about a turning-point in human history are literally true, and Liberalism must take them to heart. Never was it more necessary to look both far ahead and far afield, to realize that this little outpost of freedom and unforced wealth called the West, no more than one-fifth of the human race, is up for judgement. Not only for its colonies and aggressions, but also for its complacency, its commercial squalors, and its social injustices. We need to take a long, hard look at ourselves, to consider seriously the chance that our whole civilization will shortly be destroyed, unregretted by many men of goodwill. All political programmes must be framed *sub specie aeternitatis*. If Toynbee and Spengler really are wrong, they must be shown to be so by practical policies here and now. It is entirely possible that such policies cannot be formulated. It is very probable they will not be applied. There is much room for effort, some for hope, none for optimism.

'Where there is no vision the people perish.' Today only Communists have a real vision. It is certainly a great advantage to them, and it is certainly the West that is perishing. Let us then rival their boldness, and recognize that our ultimate vision of society is a primary weapon in the Cold War. Communists – 'bloody-minded professors' in Sir Winston Churchill's memorable and revealing phrase – are entranced by a doctrine of the ultimate future, a sort of economic Science Fiction we call Full Communism. To them it is highly attractive, though to a Liberal it is utterly repugnant. What have we to set against it? Do we need anything at all?

Their vision is of a society so rich and so productive that all restraints have faded away; for evil and tension have in their view only an economic base, and forcible restraints ('the State') will not be required when the classless, prosperous economy has sufficiently established itself. Yet since only collectivism can produce such wealth the economy is still centrally planned, being administered by a non-coercive, voluntary association. Nor does collectivism stop short at production: the means of consumption are also enjoyed in common, the individualism of the private car, for instance, yielding to the socialism of the car pool. Men are more versatile and less specialized than in the present-day economy: the differences between town and country, intellectual work and manual work, disappear, so that all are truly equal even in that most basic of all aspects, the contribution of their labour.

All receive incomes according to their needs, and work for the joy of working alone. Consequently – bearing in mind that the economy is centrally planned anyway – there is no need for money, and it, like the 'state', withers away. The general picture is of a spontaneously harmonious and uniformly depersonalized social order.

It is far from an ignoble vision, and the Communists take it very seriously indeed. They are trying here and now to put it into practice, and not all of it is as impracticable as may seem. However that is not here our concern.[1] We here ask, is an individualist economy of extreme affluence possible? Or desirable? Can we have something to aim at like Full Communism?

A view, however vague, on this subject could give us that vital sense of direction we at the moment lack: it functions, indeed, as the ill-starred American Statement of National Purpose[2] was supposed to function. It is easy to be cynical, but surely the whole idea of a Statement of National Purpose or long-term party programme is not ridiculous. Plainly, basic Communist documents are just such statements, and so too was the idea of the City of God in the Middle Ages, or the original Islamic programme of world conquest and mass conversion. Tacit agreement on how society ought to be now is not enough: we need fairly explicit agreement on what it ought to become. Indeed such agreement may well be easier to obtain.

Can there, then, be other forms of Extreme Affluence than Full Communism? We answer by asking three more questions:

(i) Is indefinite economic growth likely? For clearly only so can Full Communism or any form of Extreme Affluence be achieved.
(ii) Can any type of organization achieve it, or only some?
(iii) What are the *natural* economic and social consequences of Extreme Affluence in a democratic, capitalist society? Could they be described as Full Communism?

It is my thesis that 'Capitalism' will in fact autonomously grow into something more desirable than Full Communism, without

[1] The reader is referred to my *Political Economy of Communism*, Oxford (1962), chh. 17–20.
[2] *New York Times* (18 Sep. 1960); it was drawn up by a committee of Wise Men appointed by President Eisenhower.

any intervening nonsense of 'Socialism', 'Proletarian Revolution', and the rest, if only it is left in peace.

The merely technological side, question (i), we shall have to assume.[1] That leaves, however, (ii) the institutional side. If indefinite economic growth is possible at all, is it possible through the market, and with our present capitalist organization and political democracy?

That it should be possible without a command economy but through the market, if only by means of market socialism, is easily shown. Central physical planning has only one *intrinsic* advantage for growth over other models, and that not a decisive one: the incentive constituted by the plan targets themselves (for if the planners screw these up year by year, they put the force of law behind increases in output). In theory the mere volume of investment depends on the thrift of the people or the strength of the government, not the institutional structure of the economy. For it is as easy to extract savings from the population by taxes as by a physical plan that provides for a great deal of investment goods and few consumption goods. In either case this is mainly a political problem: of imposing abstinence on the unwilling population.

A market is more necessary the more decisions are decentralized, and this depends on the size of decision-making unit that technique imposes. Now the trend of technical progress is no longer so obviously towards yet more centralization. Marx could always effectively jeer at Proudhon: how would he run a railway? The modern liberal has a retort: how would Marx run a million motor-cars?[2] Indeed if the future is with the personal helicopter we may go still farther, for motor-roads require a large central planning body in their building if not in their use, but the air is there already. Or take the supply of power. When the industrial revolution began, it was practically synonymous with the concentration of artisans into a single building where their machines all ran off a single source of power: first water, then steam. Electricity takes us in two directions from the position thus

---

[1] Cf. Wiles, op. cit., ch. 19.

[2] Throughout the world people of a left-wing complexion are almost invariably hostile to private motor-cars and even to road haulage, in all matters where they conflict with railways. No wonder, for the motor-car came after the railway, and is the principal demonstration that time is not necessarily on their side, and that technical progress is sometimes right-wing.

achieved: its own supply is by technical necessity vastly more centralized than that of water or steam, but its use can be almost as decentralized as that of man- or bullock-power. Full many an obsolescent craftsman, or do-it-yourself enthusiast in his basement, depends on the electric grid. Undoubtedly society will never be so technically decentralized again as before the industrial revolution, but in which direction is it moving at the moment?

But even when the size of the decision-making unit does increase the market still has functions to perform in that each large enterprise produces many products, and must choose between them. The simplicities of textbook economics, which deals with one product per diagram, entirely obscure this basic point. Furthermore, large enterprises produce things for themselves, since they tend to be vertically integrated; they thus need *internal* criteria of choice. Planning could provide these two kinds of criterion, after various technical developments have taken place. At present it cannot; and even when it can, it might not perhaps show such serious advantages over a market as to make us wish to sacrifice our social structure.

Technology, therefore, shows some bias against the market mechanism, but not a big one. It certainly does not go far enough to show that indefinite economic growth technically entails collectivism.

It *is* however necessary for any economy aiming at Extreme Affluence within measurable time to grow fast. This means at least to maintain full employment and to force the overall volume of investment. Now while this is entirely compatible with a free market in everything else, political freedom is quite certainly a brake here. Thus the allocation of the enlarged investment fund can be according to profit, and indeed in private hands; and the consumer remains sovereign over the smaller slice of the cake left to him. Moreover, since the cake expands more rapidly, his smaller slice comes to represent more cake in absolute terms. But will he vote for this programme?

In that great right-wing anarchy, the USA, there is serious and successful opposition even to such a trivial strengthening of central power as is needed for perpetual full employment. And a forced volume of investment is more difficult still. To accommodate it to Western institutions with least damage to them, we need, as we see below, heavy taxation, the accumulation of a large 'above the line' surplus in the budget, and its disposal by a public investment board to public or private capital-users. The really difficult item, of course, is the higher taxes, i.e. the increase in the abstinence of the population; and this is, to repeat, a function of the power of the government, and hardly at all of the economic order.

But Western democracy means letting economic agents do more or less what they like, and therefore tolerating many comfortable abuses, restrictive practices, and traditional ways of carrying on that have little or nothing to do with the volume of abstinence. We must consider how serious these really are. First accept the pessimistic assumption that few of them could be abolished without a dictatorship; then I believe that, paradoxically, most of our economically inefficient institutions can be tolerated.

For we must distinguish most carefully between institutions that reduce the *level* of productivity ('handicaps') and those that retard its *rate of growth* ('brakes'). This distinction can best be explained in terms of its most important application, which is to the structure of agriculture. The small farm is obviously less efficient than the large, and the 'institution' of the family farm with capitalistic ownership keeps farms small. Nay, in many cases it actually diminishes them by parcellation, if younger sons cannot find work off the land and primogeniture is not the rule. But the vast bulk of agricultural improvement is independent of scale, being concerned with the qualities of seeds or the utilization of new, vertically disintegrated, special services (such as artificial insemination). It is incontestable that if we in Britain amalgamated our farms on a large and brutal scale – whether into state-farms or into private latifundia makes little difference, of course – we would increase agricultural productivity *once for all*. But the political presuppositions are quite other-worldly, and indeed specifically undemocratic. For more important than the enterprise's freedom to choose its own price and output is its freedom to decide its own internal structure. What we may call 'institutional *laissez-faire*' is one of the most important of all democratic freedoms, and it is simply arbitrary and immoral to deprive farmers of a way of life which they love and which yet makes them an *adequately* productive food base for a progressive economy. So there is no reason why we should not accept the *handicap* of our farm *structure* provided we remove the *brake* of too little farm *investment*. If we choose to grow from a lower point we will nevertheless get there in the end. Indeed, how big *is* the handicap? How much would farm amalgamation lower agricultural costs? By 10%? – who wants a bloody revolution for the price of four years' growth?

Some institutional inefficiencies, then, are brakes and some are only handicaps, and it is of the utmost importance to know which is which. I have suggested that by a merciful dispensation of providence the ones with deepest social roots are mostly handicaps. Upon the rightness of this generalization nearly everything turns, and we must take a few more examples before leaving the subject of 'brakes versus handicaps'.

Moderate protectionism is a most interesting case of a handicap that, so far from being a brake, is often actually an accelerator. Protection is, of course, a handicap in that it reduces the efficiency of the current allocation of resources; but it is also an accelerator for at least two reasons. The first is the 'infant industry' argument, which is too well known to be enlarged upon. The second reason is that free trade is deflationary. Now at least a mild inflation indubitably accelerates growth, so that we have here a very strong contrast between rates of change and absolute levels. 'For instance,' as I have said elsewhere:[1]

an attempt to quantify the advantages of free trade and inflation respectively might run thus in a given case. Suppose that 25% of the gross national produce (GNP) benefits from protection, and costs in this sector of the economy average 20% above the costs of potential imports in home currency. If protection were abolished, factors would be diverted to exports. Let these have constant costs. Then so far the economy stands to gain by 20% of 25% = 5% of the GNP. But free trade brings with it a need for greater deflation, international liquidity, adaptability to foreign demand, etc. This need is permanent and will reduce employment by say 1%. Let this mean a loss of 0·75% of the GNP (marginal factors being less efficient than the average). Also free trade worsens the terms of trade; let this reduce the GNP by a further 0·25%. Then in a static economy free trade is far better (4% better) than full employment through protection. But the same deflation, liquidity, etc., reduces also the

[1] In *Europe and the Europeans*, ed. Max Beloff (1957), p. 221.

rate of growth of the economy by say 0·5% p.a., since they entail less investment and occasional actual setbacks in current output. Then, in eight years mild inflation shows itself superior to free trade, in the particular country, and given all the circumstances.

Thus a 'handicap' is not without incidental influence on the speed of advance, nor doubtless can a 'brake' be altogether dissociated from the absolute position of the starting point. In other words, many influences play both parts.

Perhaps the most interesting case is restrictive practices, including trade unions, cartels and the withholding of new knowledge by patents. These on inspection turn out also to be only handicaps. Invention goes on, technique after new technique is developed; what happens to a country or industry that refuses to adopt them? It simply stagnates, becoming more and more backward, until finally the dam bursts. No restrictive practice lasts for ever, and then one of two things must happen. First, it may go straight for the most advanced technique available. At this point it benefits from all the usual 'advantages of immaturity', and grows faster than those who have kept up all the time; reaching, moreover, the same point in absolute development as they over the same long period. Over the average of all industries such a country will, of course, suffer a lag, but it is unlikely to increase or diminish. Or secondly, the restrictive practices merely impose a permanent lag in techniques, the adoption of every successive innovation being delayed in each industry. This obviously has not even a temporary effect on the rate of growth. Only if, thirdly, the technical lag increases all the time do restrictive practices become a brake as well as a handicap. I.e. they must become more and more restrictive for growth to be slowed.

The principal brake, then, is a low volume of investment. For technical lags can be caught up in giant strides, or if kept constant are irrelevant to the speed of growth. But if the national capital is not increased in a given year, this simply leaves us with the task of greater saving and investment next year. That apart, a free economy and society seem to suffer mainly from handicaps. The superiority of Communist growth is, if this analysis is correct, partly due to a single continuing factor: more abstinence making possible more investment; and partly to many historically circumstanced, once-for-all factors: the exceptionally rapid removal of all the old handicaps of an under-developed economy, without permitting the new ones to arise that characterize an advanced one. And in the very long run even low investment could be only a handicap. For suppose that a high-investment economy eventually succeeds in tooling up all its workers in the most modern way; then further growth will only come from technical progress. And now suppose a low-investment economy, in which capital is made to last longer and most of it is obsolete; so that only a few workers are at any moment of time equipped in the most modern way. There is clearly nothing here to make the *average* piece of capital *more* obsolete as time passes: the technical lag is, and will remain, of a certain size. Therefore this economy too is growing at the rate of technical progress. High investment is only an advantage during that long period in which there is obsolete capital (or even in certain sectors no capital), and its rapid renewal permits a country to advance towards the technological vanguard.

It is, then, clear that different forms of Extreme Affluence are technically possible. To Full Communism will be opposed here two of these possibilities: Affluent Individualism and Affluent Socialism. The former, which I submit is what Liberal policy ought to be, offers of course the more perfect contrast. It is based simply on the notion of increasing wealth, without a revolution in economic motivation. Money, the market, and private ownership of the means of production are entirely retained, and the social services disappear as people become more and more able to support themselves[1] – not quite the same, this, as 'the state withering away'! The ideal is, as under Full Communism, a rich, fully developed individual; only this time there is no bias towards Puritanism and uniformity. And there is one other big difference: the Affluent Individualist works for himself and his family, not for society; his virtues are not self-sacrifice and enthusiasm but responsibility and self-support. He has no more 'socialist consciousness' than twentieth-century John Smith, or that regrettable survival of outmoded capitalist mentality, twentieth-century Ivan Ivanov. This, precisely, is why the market mechanism has to remain.

Affluent Socialism differs from Full Communism mainly in that,

[1] Cf. Alan T. Peacock, *The Welfare Society* (1960) (Unservile State Papers, no. 2).

COLLEGE OF THE SEQUOIAS
LIBRARY

while the government is not totalitarian, minimal demands are
yet made upon the individual for moral 'improvement'. The social
services are, however, built up and eventually engulf the market
sector: in contrast to Affluent Individualism in which the social
services are confined to the provision of a minimum for all, and
eventually wither away. Thus the question of 'socialist consciousness', i.e. of the will to work without private reward, does arise.
But Affluent Socialism being less in a hurry than Full Communism, simply permits the falling will to work to slow up the rate
of growth.

It may well be asked: why have Affluent Socialism at all? Surely
the choice lies between the two extremes, the one quick-growing
but totalitarian, the other both preserving political and creating
economic freedom.[1] The writer himself can see no advantage in
Affluent Socialism, but feels it must be included: first in order to
show that there are many practicable models of Affluence;
and secondly because many people find individualism as morally
repulsive as totalitarianism. Such people should be consoled with
the prospect of a genuine third way, though one cannot help
asking why they need it.

Why, after all, is collectivism more moral than individualism?
Charity is moral, the succour of the needy; and if there are many
needy charity must be collectivized, or it will not be big enough.
Thus all Liberal talk of the 'withering away of the welfare state'
must be referred to the far future, when there really is no poverty.
Though we should prepare for such a 'withering' at the present
time by refusing to add frills to the social services, and by allowing
people to 'contract out', it is also our duty to expand the basic
provisions in a number of very expensive ways. But when there
are no needy, all this falls to the ground. Collectivism without
charity has no visible charms. It is good to work for society if
society is helping the poor. But it is rather silly to set up all these
centralized pooling arrangements otherwise. It remains, of course,
altruistic, but what superiority over individualism has the altruism
of one millionaire for another?

---

[1] It will be observed that I do not fall into the trap of equating a free market
with economic freedom. Economic freedom is a nebulous and troublesome concept.
It either means freedom from material anxiety, i.e. great wealth and leisure, or
freedom to 'do what I like with my own'. On the former definition it is assured by
any form of Extreme Affluence. On the latter it arises from a *combination* of affluence
and a free market; only the rich can have it, since only they have any 'my own' to
do 'what I like with'.

This is an awkward question, more suitable to the theologian or politician than to the economist. Such a one may be pardoned, however, for asking whether sometimes ethical judgements are not unconsciously predicated upon contingent circumstances. Female chastity seemed good before contraceptives: now one begins to wonder. So also economic altruism – we do not here speak of altruism in other respects – may possibly be found to rest on the assumption that there is in fact poverty. Or again, to attribute to central planning some moral superiority over the market – or vice versa – is surely too absurd and eccentric for serious consideration. These two different ways of allocating resources seem to me morally quite neutral. When – as is surely inevitable – they one day become equally efficient the choice between them will be political: the more decentralized is the more compatible with personal freedom.

Moreover, Affluent Socialism would appear gratuitously to raise the question of the will to work of unpaid men: and thus to impale itself deliberately on the dilemma: economic stagnation or totalitarianism. For a Communist government, with its propaganda and its Komsomol, might well instil the will to work unpaid into its subjects. But a Socialist government clearly could not.

Not that Extreme Affluence was ever an ideal of such people, but rather the very moderate, petty bourgeois level of living described, for instance, by William Morris in his *News from Nowhere*. The limited aspirations of this book demand careful study by Liberals. For if we have to deal with Communism abroad, we also compete with our own native socialists at home, and Morris's old book epitomizes to this day many of their inmost ideals. In Morris's Utopia there is indeed no money, but the virtuous citizenry are content with a pipe of tobacco and a row on the Thames. Moreover, there goes with this economic abstemiousness a whole William Morris culture or society. In his review of Raymond Williams's *Long Revolution* (1961), Mr Richard Wollheim describes the latter succinctly: '. . . what, in contrast to the American Dream, the ideal of affluent and assertive individualism, might be called the English Dream: the ideal of the collective unalienated folk society, where honest men work together and create together, the ideal of Ruskin and William Morris and Leavis. Born of Nonconformity, it has only too easily shown itself indifferent to the values of nonconformity with a small "n"".[1]

Clearly of all parties, Conservative and Communist included, the Labour Party is the one least in tune with the problems of Extreme Affluence.

Now it is obvious that a society of individualists in a market economy could not reproduce the institutional arrangements of Full Communism. Communists will doubtless be delighted with this admission, but are they wise to rejoice? Surely, on the contrary, their own plan for Extreme Affluence is grim in the extreme, and a bold Western propaganda has much to offer in the field of Extreme Affluence just because Full Communism can be avoided. Taking some sensible mixture of Affluent Individualism and Affluent Socialism we can say:

(*a*) Distribution according to need is already far advanced in Western capitalism, which shows no fewer social services, and very much better ones, than any Communist country. Moreover the 'social service' approach to distribution according to need is not the only, nor in Liberal opinion the best. The alternative is some form of co-ownership or 'people's capitalism', in which the capital itself – i.e. the private ownership of the means of production – is 'distributed according to need'. The individual can then fall back on his own capital and decide his own needs. He thus escapes from the probably totalitarian consequences of submission to a central authority that decides what he needs.

(*b*) Money will not wither away, but this is in no sense a disadvantage. The prejudice against money is absurd and has no intellectual basis. It is absolutely vital as an alternative to compulsion, in any remotely likely society.

(*c*) Many of the items in Full Communism are soulless and humourless, delighting in uniformity for its own sake. In particular, the difference between town and country is a delight to all, and the very stuff of life to many. There are, by nature and nurture, urban and rural types, and urban and rural phases in the life of an average man. Extreme Affluence would enable these demands to be met far more fully than at present; as indeed all other demands for differentiation. There is no case

---

[1] *Spectator* (10 March 1961).

for deliberately assimilating the internal structure of the farming enterprise to that of a factory: many people *like* small personal enterprises, the present structure of capitalist farming caters to a genuine human need. It is tyrannical to try to alter both the farm and the farmer. Moreover, the undoubted cost of small-scale family farming in efficiency is offset by the economic cost of compulsory collectivization, the unpopularity of which makes it equally inefficient. The correct way out is the natural, voluntary, American way: the heavily capitalized medium-scale family farm. In a word, Affluent Individualism would preserve the *institutional laissez-faire* that Full Communism would destroy. This is an unmixed blessing.

(*d*) The further collectivization of consumption is a monstrous objective, having no economic necessity and exactly contrary to many tendencies within any Affluent Society. Indeed we may boldly generalize about the present trend of technical progress as follows: it at no point actually favours small-scale operation, since small units can always be reduplicated and large-scale management of such combinations is an established technical possibility.[1] But it may quite well operate less sharply against small-scale units at some times than at others, and especially so if there is urgent demand for inventions suitable to small units, so that research is directed that way. Now it so happens that all over the world two small economic units have immense social advantages and traditional prestige: the family and the family farm. Their obstinate survival has created those deeply un-Marxian objects, the individual washing-machine and the rotavator. The loss in efficiency compared with the laundry and the large tractor is perceptible but not tragic. And in any case the loss is only a 'handicap', not a 'brake'; technical progress is as likely in these small things as in big ones. In a word, if people like to live that way they can certainly afford it. If they lose a decade or so in their march towards the economic Utopia they at least do not lose sight altogether of other human values, unknown to Full Communism.

(*e*) It is not only Puritanism and uniformity from which those suffer who live under Communism. The very generalized

[1] I.e. the L-shaped long average cost curves is in a sense an *a priori* law. See my *Price, Cost, and Output*, 2nd edn., Oxford (1961), p. 220.

feeling of constraint and effort makes the whole of economic activity unpleasant. The tension, the straining after goals in a command economy, is the main item here: it takes enjoyment out of work at all levels, and encourages corruption, the cutting of corners, etc. A man should be happy while he works; and this matters because work is such a large part of his life.

So even if we look into the farthest future, more liberal systems of economy, while necessarily less dynamic, *can* be made dynamic enough given the will, and are on all other grounds vastly superior.

'Can' is of course the operative word. *Will* we? It is not enough to assert that a capitalist economy has a right to survive, and will surely bring forth at the End of Things a better kind of man. For the End of Things is a long way off, and in the meantime there is the Cold War, in which dynamism ranks not indeed above all other desiderata, but very high. Buoyed up, then, by our vision, and moving in general towards it, may we yet not be forced to deviate from it in particular? And will we have the energy and courage either to pursue the vision or to deviate strongly enough if necessary? I proceed from the assumption that we must fight the Cold War on all the three fronts of foreign policy mentioned on p. 43: we need foreign aid *and* missiles *and* an exemplarily just society; i.e. both redistribution and rapid growth. Different assumptions would produce different answers.

To establish social justice, it is commonly thought we must sacrifice growth, since men both work and save more if there is inequality. But how true is this? Take first saving. It is well established that the rich save a greater proportion of their incomes than the poor, so that any transference of income from rich to poor leads, *ceteris paribus,* to less saving overall. But how much does this quantitatively matter? Capitalism suffers bouts of unemployment, which government policy can cure more easily the *less* saving there is at such times. Most savings in any case are made nowadays not by individuals but by corporations, whose abstinence is scarcely at all dependent on how rich their shareholders are. And finally the government, through its budget surplus 'above the line', can save great quantities: not indeed with ease, but as easily as a rich man. So this argument for inequality remains valid, but is of scarcely any importance any more.[1]

As to work, one wonders whether inequality ever did promote it. The most striking contrast today is between the leisurely proletariat before its telly and the hard-working bourgeoisie with its bulging brief-case. Now one might say that this new distribution of leisure is due to the smaller income-gap between them: the rich work harder because they feel their loss, the poor less hard because they feel their gain. But a closer examination dispels this analysis. The poor work less, not because they are more equal to the rich, but because they are better off. They are simply and straightforwardly under less economic compulsion to work, and more able to afford leisure and its enjoyment. As to the rich, they too are better off than before the war.[2] They mostly enjoy their work, and there may also be some sociological change here. That bulging brief-case has become a status symbol. The drone and the playboy are very *mal vus* in rich circles – indeed their modern counterpart is more the working-class teddy boy, living on his parents and the unemployment pay he once qualified himself to draw.

In a word, the incentives to work are a minefield into which the economist, or at least the believer in *homo economicus,* walks at his peril. As the poor get richer they have *in recent decades* done less work. Equality seems to have little to do with it, mere wealth much, sociology still more. But how about the means to equality, the high and progressive income tax? Now it is true that Communism, with no or low income tax, very high purchase tax and – above all – substantial control over the gross incomes initially received, finds it far easier to reconcile equality with the incentive to work. Yet one can exaggerate the effect of our income tax. For whatever reason, as we have just seen, its climb to its present levels has coincided with an *increase* in upper-class willingness to work. Partly, no doubt, this is due to evasion, and evasion should

[1] A similar argument is that only rich men will make risky investments with their savings: the poor have to have security. But a large corporation or the government can consolidate many risks, and thus not feel any of them. And this is what actually happens: there is no evidence at all that fewer risky projects are engaged in nowadays.

[2] Official statistics, that neglect tax evasion, expense accounts, and the effect on the price-index of the tremendous number of new consumer goods, are perfectly useless in this context. We must take as witness instead such simple and incontrovertible evidence as the expansion of private schooling and foreign travel. If the rich were worse off, as they often claim, these luxuries would have shrunk.

be stopped. But partly it is due to all sorts of semi-rational factors. Thus the surtax is paid once a year in arrears; so one is for ever working hard to pay off last year's surtax, and one discounts rather heavily the prospect of paying tax on one's present work next year. Or again, a man with very fixed financial commitments or desires to consume will actually work harder even when a progressive income tax is imposed on him. Moreover, such mitigations apply to a progressive expenditure tax, and to any other substitute which would have broadly the same effects.

Heavy taxes bring huge disadvantages in the field of law-enforcement and public morality. They also distort the distribution of resources.[1] But it is highly questionable whether the particular ones we now bear lower the will to work. There is not space here for tax reform: enough to say that no alternative to our present system is an obvious improvement. Think how many conditions a tax system must fulfil: not to discourage work, not to distort the distribution of resources, to be flexible, to be just, to be difficult to evade and easy to administer, to raise lots of revenue ... we may be best off, on balance, with what we have. I conclude that if social justice means more equality – and it certainly does to me – it is compatible with rapid economic growth, even granted a substantially unchanged tax system. Nor does history contest this verdict. The absolute equality of Lenin's USSR did indeed yield to Stalin's unequal wage policy; but in the interregnum of the NEP, wages were modestly unequal while growth was very rapid, and now again, with rather greater equality, growth remains rapid. To turn to capitalism, which is more relevant: if Britain shows rather equal distribution and stagnates, USA shows inequality and also stagnates; and among the rapid 'growers' of the late nineteenth century we may contrast Sweden with Japan.

Descending to specifics, Mr Eltis in Part 3 mentions many measures that a Liberal government should take. Characteristically for one taking a less extreme view of economic growth than the present author, he thinks mainly in switches of resources: take capital from the railways and invest it more profitably, divert research funds from prestigious blind alleys, and so on. He seems

---

[1] Clearly less is produced of heavily than of lightly taxed articles, and this diminishes consumer's sovereignty. Less clearly, but of equal importance, high income taxes render employers careless of cost; and tend to drive them abroad, or into bogus expense accounts. It even pays, in special circumstances, to incur a loss, to offset against other profits.

to recommend only one extra government expenditure: on education. To my way of thinking, Britain's situation is by no means so easy, and the possibility of rapid growth without more effort and more 'planning' remote. It is true that improved use of our existing resources would help, but it is surely still more true that greater capital resources should be mobilized. Since long experience shows that the free individual does not save very much, the government must save for him. A disagreeably large 'above-the-line' budget surplus is surely a *sine qua non*.

Such a surplus, constantly disbursed upon investment projects, need not lead to the gradual socialization of the economy. In years of private investment boom, it need only be used to redeem the national debt: capital thus put on to the stock exchange will be taken off by private borrowers. Effectually the government saves and the private sector invests. In other years, such funds as are not thus taken up must indeed be invested in government projects or the existing nationalized industries – but not at low rates of return or in general on non-commercial principles, as Mr Eltis shows. Enterprises thus formed need not remain in public hands: equity capital in them, amounting to only a few per cent of the total invested, can be created by the government and sold off, while the government continues to hold only fixed debt. And since such holdings confer no control, such an enterprise would be essentially capitalistic. Central and local government can also use the surplus to erect housing, which can similarly be sold to private individuals.

Such direct state investment naturally competes with, and depresses the profits of, private enterprise in similar jobs. But it keeps employment full in the short run,[1] raises productive capacity in the long run, and thus alters the general ambience for all private investment. Thus if such a policy be accepted as a settled thing, there will be more and not less private investment. Moreover such a proposal is easily married to the pure Keynesian measures Mr Eltis recommends: should unemployment occur even so, the 'below the line' investment programme should be increased or tax revenues diminished, to bring about the required budget deficit – and vice versa for inflation. The 'Keynesian' variations

---

[1] A large budget, even though balanced, has a small 'multiplier' effect, i.e. raises aggregate demand beyond what it would have been with a small budget, also balanced.

from budgetary balance should simply be about a budget that normally includes far more government investment than at present.

There is too, at least as things are today, much that the government can do with such a surplus which does not compete with any private activity: road building, the Channel Tunnel, hospitals, education. The principal thing however is that there be action of some kind. It is too evident that private enterprise will produce no permanent investment boom; but the issue must not go by default.

A second radical measure for increased growth suggests itself; this one also not wholly disruptive of free enterprise, but inspired by Communist practice. The use of an invention by others must be cheaply licensed from the moment the patent is applied for, on pain of its refusal. Nothing in our economy is quite so obsolete as the patent system, which was clearly designed for a far slower rate of technical progress. It is a crime that technical knowledge should be withheld at all, and nowadays the thirteen-year period is ludicrously too long – the invention is normally quite out of date by then, and meanwhile lack of the knowledge that it embodies inhibits competitors from further research. Indeed, where possible, it would be better to restore our own war-time system: official awards to inventors, all technical improvements instantly become public property, no patents at all.[1]

Third and last we must mention trade unions. Britain needs a strong Taft-Hartley Act. Never was a field so packed with legal abuses, legislative connivances, surrenders of principle and general inconsistencies. And all to ensure, not the welfare of the very poor, but the continuance in their present jobs and privileges of the already well organized and quite well off. It is true that union restrictions, like our patent system, are a 'handicap' and not a 'brake'. But *what* a handicap! And on the political side the minor oppressions, the sendings to Coventry, the stuffed ballots, all cry urgently for reform.

Into this large and controversial subject one either enters fully or not at all. Let me merely point out the extreme improbability, under present circumstances, of stable prices when there is full employment and rapid growth. The unions will surely not accept a national wages policy tough enough for that until their

---

[1] It is a happy thing that the spread of government research and in private industry of mutual patent licensing has much reduced this obstacle. But it is still there.

legal powers have been curtailed. Nor can that be the only way to reform; for there is not, after all, so very much that the law of a democratic state can do to prevent men combining to raise their wages. Beside the more perfect distributive justice on which Mr Eltis insists, and the beneficent effects of more rapid growth, it is necessary above all to meet extravagant wage claims in their own field: by resisting strikes until they collapse. For the main reason why wages outstrip productivity is simply union bargaining power: let the community (and it is not hypocrisy to substitute 'community' for 'employer') then exert *its* bargaining power.

So much for growth. But economics is, or should be, also about the quality of life. So, too, should be Liberalism, and indeed politics generally. We have been too long preoccupied with the stale old questions of ownership, poverty, and social justice. However important they all were – and many of them actually remain – they do not exhaust the obstacles to a Good Society, nor even the responsibilities of government.

Take first advertising and the mass media. The accustomed eye sees past the neon signs and the pornography stands, the dulled ear lets the soap operas and commercials drone on unheeded. Yet a civilization is intolerable that demands blinkers and ear-plugs, and when every now and again these cease to insulate us we feel aesthetic pain. Or worse, we are brought up to believe it could not be otherwise, and that these things are not in fact debilitating, trivial, and false.

In passing value-judgements on these things and recommending action against them, I am fully aware I am arrogating unusual powers. Not only the economist, with his often hypocritical 'I am only a technician', but also the politician, reluctant to stir sleeping hornets, likes to steer clear of the cultural field. We all of us make value-judgements about social justice far more freely than about the style of the popular press. And yet a civilization is judged almost equally by each. If USSR has no *Guardian* at least it has no *Daily Mirror*: why then do we think its press is worse than ours? Is the political lie so obviously a greater crime than the mawkishness, the hypocritical semi-pornography, the triviality? I make, then, the usual harsh judgement of the intellectual upon most of our mass media and nearly all our advertising; only I do not apologize for doing so, or shrink from demanding action.

This debasement is due to the interaction of two forces: unrestrained profit-seeking and the tastes of *most* of the citizenry. Under Communism, where these forces are inoperative, these particular kinds of ugliness are absent; and to any fair-minded person of even moderate taste this must appear a great advantage over us. The evil has been tolerated too long, partly by our inertia and partly through an intellectual confusion: we seem to think that freedom of thought and publication is the same thing as the freedom of advertising and the mass media. In the former case the necessity to make a profit and follow tastes is a mere restraint: the essence and the motive is to say what one means, and it is rightly held that democracy depends on it. The freedom of entertainers and advertisers, however, was far from Milton's mind when he wrote *Areopagitica,* or from Mill's when he wrote *On Liberty*. It was utterly unconsidered in the tennis court at Versailles and in Independence Hall, Philadelphia. It is as if one were to call the police away from a lynch-mob on the grounds of freedom of assembly. There are of course many marginal cases and subtle inter-connections, but on the whole one could abolish advertising and beautify the mass media with only gain to political freedom. They are mere trades, and should be as subject to restriction as any other trade.

Why has *laissez-faire* worked so badly in this sphere? It is not that competition forces us to satisfy only majority tastes: for that is quite plainly untrue in all trades. It is often very profitable indeed to differentiate one's product and be one of the few, or better still the only, supplier of a minority market.[1] It is true to some extent that the minority cannot afford what it wants. For instance, not even the vast egghead population of Greater New York can render a decent television channel profitable. But, on the whole, eggheads are rich, and it is worth while supplying their tastes in a competitive economy. They like to complain, say, about the shortening of the broadcasting hours of the Third Programme. But on balance, what with the LP, the Phaidon Press, and the paperback, they have done very well. Technical progress does not discriminate against intellectuals, and a competitive, profit-motivated economy willingly provides them with its fruits. Their fathers would envy them greatly.

---

[1] One exception here: the BBC. Long technically constrained to offer only three audio programmes, it could indeed hardly justify the broadcasting of any programme that served less than 100,000. But now that we have FM there is no technical restraint on the number of audio channels.

It is rather misleading to raise the question in this form. What we are really asking is why the majority product is as vulgar and debased as it is? Were no minority product conceivable, this would still be a problem. Indeed we must further enquire why the minority product is often subject to a parallel debasement. Why must the organ of the Establishment appeal so nakedly to the lower natures of its élite readers? (I refer to the advertisement, Top People Take The Times.) It is not a question of majorities versus minorities, but of general and progressive debasement of standards, particularly in the approach of advertisers and entertainers to the majority.

I suggest that we face here a historically unique, once-for-all process, brought about indeed by competition and the profit motive, but exceptional. Advertising and the mass media began, effectually, in the nineteenth century: a period of unusually high moral tone and general public standards. (The cynic may emphasize 'tone' and 'public' if he wishes; it does not alter the point.) The entrepreneurs in this field have progressively discovered how lustful and irrational people are, how most cheaply and effectually to persuade and amuse them. At every turn the higher standards and the greater restraint have been discovered to be less *profitable* than the lower standards and the less restraint. With a relaxation of public morals, the law, and police activity, competition has done its work. But had sheer profit not pointed the way, the relaxation of public morals would have been without effect; after all, masses of people are still willing to pay for good, clean fun, and they get it. Moreover we are probably not far from bottom by now: women cannot be nuder than nude, the number of sexual perversions one can portray is limited, horror films have been tried and on the whole abandoned, without censorship. In politics one can even say we are past the turn; the level of sophistication has risen and Northcliffe's rabble-rousing would fall flat today.

This last example shows clearly that supply and demand can raise as well as lower the standards of advertising and the mass media, without any form of public regulation. But still the *dégringolade* of the last hundred years has been frighteningly complete, standards are now intolerably low, and it would be fatuous complacency to expect them to revert to decency under their own steam, either soon or indeed ever. Besides, low standards perpetuate themselves. They reinforce the tastes that created them.

There can be no doubt that the New Left are wrong in attributing them to a capitalist conspiracy, or in assigning the role of injured innocence to the proletarian consumer. But in this at least they are right: the proletarian consumer will not emerge from his debasement of his own accord. Thus the question arises, *Is cultural* laissez-faire *really right*?

Grasping this nettle recently, Mr Irving Kristol[1] has said that it is not, and has demanded government intervention. It would take us too far afield to be very specific here, since there are so many special situations. The one worthwhile generalization is that the climate of opinion should be changed. Advertising and the mass media should be recognized not as laughable excrescences on a healthy body, but as serious diseases. They reinforce those evil tendencies from which they spring: materialism, triviality, taste-lessness, snobbery, and lust. If the Good Society is innocent of Puritanism, and welcomes all kinds of pleasure, including especially pleasure in the sexual act, it will certainly not welcome them in the form and style in which they are now commonly presented. *Moreover our competitors the Communists are already much closer to the Good Society in these respects.* Admittedly they have fallen into the opposite trap of Puritanism, but they are at least now making a serious effort to emerge from it. We are making no effort at all to emerge from ours.

So the first general task is to awaken a sense of urgency. But it would be cowardly not to be specific at all. I would therefore propose these concrete measures for Britain at the present time:

(i) More lay members on the Press Council, and statutory powers for it over newspaper owners, including that of com-pulsory divestiture when monopoly threatens in any field.

(ii) Journalism be constituted a profession like medicine; there should be qualifying examinations for journalists, a 'Hippo-cratic Oath', and the ever-present danger of 'disbarment' for unprofessional conduct.

These two proposals start from the belief that the modern monopoly journalist, whether owner or reporter, wields tremen-dous power by reason of the scale and the expertness of his operation; it is an anachronism to leave him uncontrolled as if he

[1] 'High, Low, and Modern', *Encounter* (1961).

were merely Daniel Defoe, but direct governmental control is too
dangerous.

(iii) All regulations under (i) and (ii) include saving clauses
designed to exempt political activity and political comment
(but not political reporting).

(iv) Advertisers on ITV be deprived of the right to choose the
time of day or day of the week when their advertisement is
shown. These should be balloted for. In this way we remove
even the indirect influence of the advertiser on the type of
programme broadcast at certain times. Naturally advertisers
would pay less for such a privilege, but the programme
companies could stand the loss very well.

(v) Pay TV be introduced immediately, at whatever cost, and
be subsidized if necessary.

(vi) All hoardings outside built-up areas be forbidden.

(vii) The activity known as editorial publicity (the influencing of
journalists and others to carry items of advertising disguised
as news and comment) should be forbidden.

(viii) All other advertising, except in newspapers and magazines,
be heavily taxed.

(ix) All advertising expenditures above £1,000 p.a. must be
channelled through recognized agencies; they may not be
handled directly by the manufacturers, trade association,
etc. These agencies receive revocable licences from the
government, which publishes a code of practice.

These items forbid the worst excrescences of the trade, and tax
the rest. They preserve however the principal vested interest: the
press, whose revenue without advertising would be most severely
cut. I admit that this exemption has nothing but expediency behind
it, but the fact remains that we would not pay double prices for
our newspapers. At a later date, when the general morality of the
advertising trade has crept up to the level at which journalism
now stands, an independent professional body should be substituted for the arrangements in (ix). Note that these proposals deal
with advertising as a moral and cultural force. Its directly economic
disadvantages are treated by Mr Eltis below.

I do not wish to insist that these particular measures are practicable. Something like them should, however, be *made* practicable.
Where there is a will there is a way. A society that has successfully

regulated drinking hours and weights and measures will not find this task beyond its administrative capacity.

One broad lesson emerges. We live in a complicated world, dangerous to our liberties both externally and internally. I say 'internally' because laissez-faire *is less efficient than we think*. It is a late nineteenth-century truism that *laissez-faire* cannot protect the poor or establish social justice: a truism that, as we have seen, the twenty-first century may refute. But if the case for *laissez-faire* will one day be strengthened there, it has meantime lost ground on other fronts. The first half of the twentieth century showed us that we need the government for full employment – and that is the Keynesian case against *laissez-faire*. The second half has shown us that we need it for growth – and that is the Marxist case. It has not proved difficult for Liberalism to swallow Keynes, who was himself a Liberal with a big L. Marx will be more indigestible.

Indeed he and his successors are the obvious antithesis of Liberalism, and most of what they say can happily be rejected out of hand. But not all: Communist economic growth is more than a threat, it is a lesson. We have a very hard row to hoe: to adopt what is good and still to keep our liberties. If there is little nationalization but heavy taxation, few direct controls but a much weaker labour movement, rapid growth but perpetually rising prices, just how much are our liberties threatened? In what concrete ways do we expose ourselves to arbitrary rule? *What* degree of economic *laissez-faire* is the required minimum for the rule of law? And as to popular culture – which is also in its way part of the Marxist case against *laissez-faire* – can it be censored or even guided without inhibitions on true reporting and free opinion?

These are essentially political questions, that I have raised but not answered. I hold them to be very specific, and subject to no blanket answer. If we shy away, if we return a quite unconstructive negative, if we let the government and our party forever refuse to grasp the nettles, then the future is with those professional graspers of nettles, the Communists.

PART THREE

Growth Without Inflation

WALTER ELTIS

The part that economic factors play in life should not, ideally, be great. Personal relationships, religion, individual freedom, and aesthetic and intellectual stimulation matter far more. But life can be intolerably difficult for millions of people if economic policy is grossly mismanaged – and it has often been mismanaged in the past fifty years. Such mismanagement can lead to political embitterment and, at times, to a readiness to support political extremes that threaten fundamental liberties, as events in Germany in the 1930s illustrate. On the positive side, a successful economic policy, by making economic security and leisure available to more and more people, enlarges the time and thought that men and women are able to devote to what is really important.

The first concern of economic policy, then, must be to avoid major mistakes which make life difficult – unemployment, inflation, balance-of-payments crises, and a proliferation of controls and interferences by the government in people's lives. A party must have a policy which protects the people of the country from such disturbances. In addition, a party can pursue a number of positive economic aims. Among the positive economic aims of the Liberal Party are its concern that Britain should have a faster rate of economic growth, and its concern to protect the interests of the consumer rather than the interests of industrial pressure groups, monopolies, and trade associations. To some extent these negative and positive aims are interconnected. For instance, the protection of the consumer at home from monopoly, from deceptive advertising, and from shoddy and unreliable goods also protects the consumer abroad by forcing businesses to improve the real quality of their products, and so it is helpful to our balance of payments position. In spite of such interconnections, it is perhaps simplest to suggest first the ways in which a Liberal government could solve the negative problems of preventing unemployment, inflation, major balance-of-payments problems, and excessive government control and interference; and, after that, to suggest ways in which it could pursue its positive economic aims. Britain's entry into the European

Common Market would create many opportunities, but it will not alter the fundamental nature of the problems which need to be solved.

PREVENTING UNEMPLOYMENT

Unemployment is mainly due either to a lack of demand for the output of the economy as a whole, or to a lack of demand for the output of certain regions. For instance, since 1948 unemployment in the United Kingdom has not exceeded 2·3% of the labour force in any year, but unemployment in Northern Ireland has exceeded 5% in every single year and even reached 10·6% in 1952. In the post-war period such unemployment as occurred in the United Kingdom was almost entirely regional. On the other hand, between 1923 and 1939 unemployment in the United Kingdom never fell below 9·7% in any single year, and it was clearly then not simply a matter of regional unemployment. Where unemployment is general, the solution is to give people all over the country more money to spend, so that more goods will be bought, and more workers employed to produce them. This can easily be achieved through the budget, either by reducing rates of taxation and so increasing the amount of money people are able to spend, while leaving government spending unchanged, so that the total amount which is spent is increased; or else by increasing government spending and leaving other kinds of spending unchanged. One of the main reasons why Keynesian solutions to the unemployment problem were resisted in this country in the inter-war period, and were resisted in America during the period of the Eisenhower administration, is that they necessarily involve a budget deficit, and so an increase in the National Debt. A reduction in taxation with unchanged government expenditure necessarily causes a deficit in the budget if it was formerly balanced. But this is the essence of the Keynesian solution to the problem of unemployment. Unemployment must be due to insufficient demand for the goods which workers produce, and so any solution to the problem must consist in causing more money to be spent on goods. If the government spends more, and takes the extra money away from people by raising rates of taxation, this does no good at all. To solve the problem, the government must spend more, or tax less, and either of these is likely to involve a budget deficit and an increase in the National Debt. This is necessarily a part of the Keynesian solution to the problem, but in Britain in the inter-war period (when a Labour Prime Minister split his party and formed a National Government to balance the budget, and so prevent the unemployment problem being solved), and in the USA until 1961, there was great concern with budget balancing. In economic policy it is important to distinguish what is of real importance from accountancy conventions, and millions of unemployed workers clearly mattered much more than the accountancy conventions which bothered Ramsay MacDonald and President Eisenhower. A Liberal government should never hesitate to maintain full employment by ensuring that enough money is always spent to maintain full employment in the economy as a whole.[1]

The problem of regional unemployment is much more difficult. If the government reduces rates of taxation, the result will be that more money will be spent throughout the economy, and so there will be too much demand for goods in those parts of the country where there is no unemployment, and prices will tend to rise there, while the unemployment situation will be alleviated in the depressed areas. Thus the regional unemployment problem would be solved at a cost of causing inflation everywhere else. A solution of a regional unemployment problem must take the form of an increase in expenditure in precisely those parts of the country where there is unemployment, or in assisted migration where the establishment of local industries is out of the question. At present the need is for greater expenditure in Northern Ireland, Wales, and Scotland. The simplest solution to the problem would be to cause a reduction in local authority rates in those parts of the country. This would be an easier solution than to have lower tax rates in those parts of the country, because hitherto tax rates have been uniform for every part of the UK, but local authority rates are in any case different in different cities and areas. It would be a very simple matter for the government to make substantial grants to councils in parts of the country where there was substantial unemployment. The councils concerned could then reduce rates and this would lead to an increase in expenditure by the people who pay rates;

---

[1] It is argued below, in the section of this chapter dealing with inflation, that full employment and stable prices are not always incompatible.

it would also encourage factories to be built in those parts of the country. In this way the problem of regional unemployment could be solved without inflation in the rest of the economy.[1] The present government has done something to alleviate the problem of regional unemployment, but a great deal clearly remains to be done. In January 1961 8·1% of the labour force was unemployed in Northern Ireland, 3·7% in Scotland, and 3·1% in Wales, and since these are the average figures, the percentage of the labour force unemployed in parts of Northern Ireland, Scotland, and Wales must have been much higher than these figures suggest.

In a Liberal economic policy, the very highest priority should be given to preventing unemployment from becoming substantial anywhere in the economy. The solution to the problem of unemployment is now well known and widely agreed to, and any government that allows it to occur on a substantial scale anywhere in the United Kingdom is guilty of negligence.

PREVENTING INFLATION

It is more difficult to prevent inflation than unemployment. A solution to the problem must first ensure that there is no demand-induced inflationary pressure. To ensure this, the total quantity of goods which people plan to buy over the coming year, for instance, must not exceed the total quantity of goods that the economy can make available for use at home in the coming year. If people try to buy more goods than the economy can supply, the excess demand will either cause a rise in prices (so that some people cannot afford to carry out their plans) or an unfavourable balance of payments (i.e. the extra goods come from abroad) or else a general shortage of goods in the shops so that people have to queue up for goods and cannot buy some of the goods they had planned to buy. To prevent inflation, balance-of-payments difficulties due to excess demand, and the kind of shortages and queues which were characteristic of the period 1945–51, the government clearly needs to keep people's plans to buy goods in line with the quantity of goods the economy is able to supply. This cannot be done perfectly by any government. Since the need is to keep plans to spend (which cannot be exactly foreseen by any government)

[1] The extra incomes in the regions of unemployment would slightly increase demand in the whole economy, but the government could counter this by slightly reducing effective demand in the economy as a whole, at the same time as the rate reductions were made in the depressed areas.

in line with what the economy will produce in the next year (which obviously cannot be forecast exactly), there will clearly almost always be an error of something like $1-1\frac{1}{2}\%$ in the two forecasts taken together. This kind of error is unavoidable, because the government has to make forecasts to decide what it will need to do to keep plans to spend in line with the quantity of goods which will be available, and no government anywhere in the world can make these forecasts exactly. If an economy has unemployment, this problem can be solved easily, because if people plan to buy more goods than the economy is currently producing, more goods will be produced; some of the unemployed workers will be brought into employment, and thus there will not be any shortage of goods, and there will be little tendency for prices to rise. In fact, because there are unemployed workers, production can always be expanded to balance demand, so it doesn't really matter how good the government forecasts are. Germany up to 1958 and the USA since 1952 have had much less inflation than Great Britain because they had quite a lot of unemployment, and so production could always be made to balance demand. This is not a solution to the problem of inflation the Liberal Party would ever wish to adopt, and a Liberal government would obviously have to solve the really difficult problem of keeping prices constant when there is no unemployment in the economy. To their credit, Conservative governments in Great Britain since 1951 have chosen to try to solve the problem of inflation without resorting to unemployment, but the way they have gone about solving this problem is open to a great deal of criticism.

Before a possible Liberal solution to this problem can be outlined, however, the full magnitude of the difficulty of preventing inflation must be explained. Let us imagine that the government has been completely successful in always keeping the quantity of goods which people plan to buy in line with the quantity of goods the economy is able to make available at full employment. We are assuming, in fact, that the difficulties of forecasting have been completely solved, and the government has succeeded in bringing buying plans and the actual potentialities of the economy into line with each other. It is still not at all certain that prices will be stable, because wages might rise more quickly than production. Wages are negotiated in many separate bargains all over the country, at all times in the year. There is no guarantee at all that wage increases will be the same as increases in production, but if they exceed increases in production the labour costs of most goods rise, and so prices tend to rise. If prices rise in one year, they tend to rise in the next year as well, because the trade unions understandably ask for particularly big wage increases so that workers' incomes can keep up with the cost of living. Thus, even if there is never any excess demand for goods in the economy, prices may rise every year because wage increases continually exceed increases in production. This latter phenomenon is generally referred to as cost-induced inflation, while a situation where people's plans to spend are excessive is referred to as a demand-induced inflation. To prevent inflation a government often has to solve both these problems, because both kinds of inflation are often present together.

When these problems are considered together, it is possible to see why the Conservative government's solution to them has been so open to criticism. They have not done anything at all to reduce the pressure of cost-induced inflation. The main measures they have used to reduce demand, higher interest rates and higher purchase tax rates, both increase costs and the cost of living. They have thus the effect of reducing one kind of inflationary pressure and increasing another kind, which is no use at all. It is not even certain that moderately higher interest rates reduce demand, because they seem hardly to affect the volume of investment, which is their 'official' function, while they increase the incomes of the people who receive the extra interest, and so their plans to spend may be increased as much as other people's are reduced. A further criticism of the use of interest rates as a method of economic control is that their effect is very slow, as well as being uncertain. The difficulty about this is that it is easier to forecast what is likely to happen in the next year than what is likely to happen in two years' time. It may be necessary to reduce spending in the next year, but to increase it in two years' time. Interest rates may well do as much harm as they do good, because they act so slowly that their effect may be exactly the opposite of what is needed by the time they are effective. What is needed is a control that has no cost push effect, that has a forecastable effect, and that works quickly. Interest rates fail from all three of these points of view, and many of our economic difficulties in recent years have been due to the fact that Conservative governments have made so much use of such a useless means of economic control.

A possible Liberal policy with regard to demand-induced inflation will now be considered. The problem here is to make accurate forecasts and to make the necessary adjustments to the level of demand in the economy which these forecasts suggest. The standard of forecasting since the war has not been helped by the very small extent to which British governments have used expert economic advice. The lack of expert economists in the Treasury and in other Ministries is disquieting, and the minor extent to which the advice of the few economists who are employed by the government is used is even more disquieting.[1] A preference for non-expert over expert advice when expert advice is available is absolutely inexcusable, and this is a state of affairs which a Liberal government should rapidly investigate and correct. The problem of altering the level of demand in the economy in the direction the forecasts suggest is mainly one of choosing the right methods of economic control. It was argued above that a control must act quickly and that its total effect must be forecastable. It was also argued that it must reduce demand without raising the cost of living at the same time. Any kind of indirect taxation, such as purchase tax or a turnover tax, would clearly raise the cost of living, because it would make the goods which were more heavily taxed more expensive, and the same criticism could be applied to a payroll tax. A payroll tax would raise the cost of labour to all employers. The main way in which a government could change the level of demand quickly without raising the cost of living at the same time would be by changing the rate of income tax. It could be argued that this is an unpleasant method to use, but a situation where people plan to buy more goods than are available is in any case unpleasant, and these plans must somehow be altered. Any method of control whatsoever must persuade people to buy less, and it is in the interests of the British people that the control should work quickly and effectively. If it works slowly and ineffectively, inflation would not be stopped, and the government might eventually have to use much more expensive and prolonged methods like the credit squeeze of 1956–9, which prevented British production from expanding for

[1] Cf. T. Balogh's chapter in *The Establishment*, ed. Hugh Thomas (1959), and P. D. Henderson in *Oxford Economic Papers* (1961).

three years, thus costing the British people about £2,000 million worth of lost production.

The great advantage of using income tax to reduce demand would be that it could work quickly, and that it would not raise the cost of living at the same time. To make income tax work quickly, two changes in the tax system would need to be made. The first is that the Chancellor of the Exchequer would need to be able to alter rates of income tax at any time – within limits laid down in the Finance Act – and not merely in the annual budget. This would obviously be necessary, because if demand needed to be reduced or increased, it would need to be changed at once, and this need would be completely frustrated if the change was always postponed until the following April. The second change which would be needed would be that people who did not pay income tax by the PAYE system would have to pay their taxes the year their income was earned, and not a year later as is frequently the case at present. This would be necessary to make changes in taxation immediately effective.

There are two further weapons a Liberal government could use to control the level of demand without raising the cost of living. The first of these is the use of Hire Purchase controls which act quickly and effectively without altering the cost of living. The second would be the use of changes in investment allowances to influence the rate of industrial investment. The Chancellor of the Exchequer would need to be able to alter these at any time in the year, and not simply in the annual budget. This might be reinforced by the introduction of a system similar to that used in Sweden to encourage firms to time their investment plans so that they do not cause fluctuations in demand. Firms could have the alternative of either paying the standard rate of tax on their profits, in which case they could invest whenever they wished, or alternatively they could pay a lower rate of tax and place their profits in a special fund which the government would release for investment when this was in the public interest. Another possible way in which the government can influence the rate of investment quickly without raising the cost of living is by controlling the period over which new industrial debentures and new local government loans must be repaid. The government would never ask firms or local authorities to repay money they had already borrowed more quickly, because this would be unjust, but it could make it illegal to float new loans where the repayment period exceeded a given number of years. This type of control would be an application to the field of investment of something very similar to the hire purchase controls which have been so effective in quickly influencing the level of consumer demand.

By using these methods, a Liberal government could alter the level of demand quickly, so that plans to spend only differed slightly from the quantity of goods available. In this way demand-induced inflation could be kept to a mimimum, and this could be done without any stimulus to cost-induced inflationary pressure.

Eliminating cost-induced inflation would be much more difficult than eliminating demand-induced inflation. There are two ways in which the problem could be approached. In the first place, a successful policy to raise the rate of economic growth might eliminate cost-push inflation. Secondly, it might be possible to persuade trade unions and employers to agree to a National Wages Policy which would not be inflationary. In Britain since the war, wages have increased on average by something like 6% a year, and output by something like $2\frac{1}{2}$% a year. Wage costs and prices have risen on average by about $3\frac{1}{2}$% a year. If output could be induced to rise more quickly, the pace of inflation might be reduced in two ways. First, if output rose by, for instance, 4% a year, and wages continued to rise by 6% a year, prices might rise by 2% a year instead of by $3\frac{1}{2}$%. Secondly, it is possible that this slower pace of inflation might lead to smaller wage demands and wage increases in the following year, since it is often argued that one object of wage demands is to compensate for the loss of income due to inflation. If, for instance, reducing the pace of inflation from $3\frac{1}{2}$% a year to 2% caused a reduction in wage increases from 6% a year to 5%, the pace of inflation might be further reduced to 1% a year. This might lead to a further fall in the pace of wage increases, and so on. Thus, any increase in the rate of growth would reduce the pace of inflation, both because it would make any given wage increase less inflationary, and because it would be likely to reduce the pace of wage increases. The problem of raising Britain's rate of growth is considered below, and the rate of cost inflation would be reduced to the extent that the policy outlined there is successful.

It is however unlikely that the rate of growth could be raised sufficiently to eliminate cost inflation altogether, and a National Wages Policy would be needed to eliminate the remainder of the inflationary pressure. It could be argued that it would be most difficult to persuade the trade unions to agree to a National Wages Policy. Conservative governments since 1951 have not succeeded in persuading the trade unions to agree to wage-restraint, and even Sir Stafford Cripps found it very difficult to persuade them to agree to wage-restraint in 1948. Even if the trade unions did agree, there would be further difficulties. A high proportion of workers in Britain negotiate for the actual wages they are paid in the factory in which they are employed. The amount they are actually paid through piece-rates, bonuses, and overtime may have only a slight connection with the wages that are negotiated at industrial and national levels. Thus, even if the trade unions agreed at the national level to limit wage increases to (for instance) 3% a year, the wages which workers were actually paid might still rise by 5% a year. Another difficulty to be overcome would be that a very prosperous industry might wish to expand, and might therefore need to raise its wages relatively to the wages paid in other industries so as to attract sufficient labour to make the expansion possible. The National Wages Policy would need to take account of this kind of problem,[1] but it would be difficult to do so in negotiations on a national scale which were largely political in character. On examination, these difficulties may prove to be much less serious than they appear at first sight.

It is not surprising that the trade unions have failed to agree to wage-restraint during the period of Conservative government. Since 1951 a series of changes in the structure of taxation have been made which have continually improved the position of property owners and surtax payers relatively to that of wage earners. In the two years 1958–60, to take an extreme example, dividends on ordinary and preference shares increased by 34%, while weekly wage rates increased by 5½% and weekly earnings by 11½%.[2] This kind of 'free for all' is naturally very discouraging to wage-restraint. A Liberal government should never attempt to

[1] A shortage of a particular kind of skilled labour, for instance draughtsmen, would present a similar problem.
[2] *Economic Survey*, HMSO (1961).

persuade the workers to agree to wage-restraint without also
ensuring that property incomes increased at a moderate rate. (The
actual relationship between the two rates of increase would
obviously be subject to negotiation.) A Conservative government
is never likely to agree to limit the rate of increase of property
incomes by anything other than exhortation, and they are therefore
never likely to persuade the workers to agree to wage-restraint.

The difficulties in persuading the trade unions to agree to
wage-restraint in the period 1945–51 were partly due to austerity
after the war, which naturally caused a large number of families
to be discontented with their incomes; but while there is much
discontent now, it is likely that it is much less extreme than it
was in the immediate post-war years. There was also probably
less realization then than now that continuous inflation may cause
severe balance-of-payments difficulties and that these are indirectly
harmful to workers by making it more difficult to maintain a high
and continuous rate of economic growth. It is likely that this is
widely understood now by the leaders of the trade unions, if not
by the rank and file, and it might now be possible to persuade the
trade unions to agree to a National Wages Policy.

It is not often realized that a National Wages Policy could
be in the economic interests of many workers. Between 1946
and 1958 the index of weekly wage rates increased by 83% while
prices increased by 74%.[1] Thus in this twelve-year period, the
purchasing power of the wages of a worker who was paid a
standard wage rate with few opportunities for piecework and
overtime increased on average by only about $5\frac{1}{2}$%. Examples
of workers in this kind of situation are railwaymen and municipal
workers. In the same period the total quantity of consumer goods
that people bought increased altogether by 28%.[1] Thus the
quantity of goods the average worker receiving a standard wage
rate could buy increased by only $5\frac{1}{2}$% in a period when the total
quantity of goods people bought altogether increased by 28%. It
would certainly seem to be in the interests of such workers to
limit the pace of wage increases if, by doing so, the cost of living
could be kept stable. The trade unionist has at present the power
to raise wages, but he has no power to control the price level, and

[1] These figures are taken from the quarterly *Bulletin of the London Cambridge
Economic Service*, which is published in the *Times Review of Industry* each March,
June, September, and December.

therefore he cannot be certain that the wage increases he can gain will raise his standard of living. If he could use his power instead to negotiate with a government which could guarantee to keep prices stable, he could be sure that any wage increase he obtained would allow him to buy more goods. He would then, in many cases, be making much better use of his power to bargain. There might thus be much more support among workers for a just National Wages Policy than is often imagined.

It is arguable that there is a very good chance that a Liberal government would be able to persuade the trade unions and the employers to implement a National Wages Policy which would not be inflationary. The problem would then be to make such a policy effective by ensuring that actual earnings did not increase faster than the nationally negotiated wage rates. It would be essential here to eliminate demand-induced inflationary pressure successfully. Providing there is no excess demand for labour in any part of the country, so that there are not more vacancies than unemployed workers in any part of the country, there is no reason why firms should need to bid against each other for labour. In this case, much of the 'wages drift' would be eliminated, and the National Wages Policy would be largely effective.[1] The successful elimination of all demand-induced inflationary pressures would also solve the problem of the industry which needed to expand its labour force. The solution of the demand problem would ensure that other industries were reducing their employment at the rate at which this industry wished to increase it, and there would therefore be no need to raise wages to attract sufficient labour.

In fact, a National Wages Policy would be both politically and economically practicable, and a Labour or Liberal Government could implement it. A Conservative government could not, because a policy of this kind would require an agreement between workers and property owners, and Conservative governments always side so obviously and openly with property owners that they are never likely to succeed in negotiating an agreement. The result is that inflation is an almost inevitable accompaniment of Conservative government, and for this reason Conservative

[1] A successful solution to the problem of regional unemployment (along the lines outlined above) would be an indispensable part of this policy, because otherwise the elimination of inflationary shortages of labour in London and the Midlands would be impossible without the creation of intolerable levels of unemployment in Scotland and Wales.

government is certainly contrary to the economic interests of people who live on salaries and fixed incomes.

Obviously a Liberal government could not keep prices exactly stable, because of the difficulties on the demand side, but it could probably prevent prices from changing by more than 1% or 1½% in most years. A Liberal government could attach major priority to price stability and full employment. Anything else it did would have to be done within the main framework of the lines of policy which have been outlined.

AVOIDING BALANCE-OF-PAYMENTS CRISES

The problem of preventing serious balance-of-payments crises is more difficult to solve than the problems of unemployment and inflation. This is because the main items in the balance of payments are naturally very responsive to economic activity in countries other than Britain, which cannot be influenced to more than a very small extent by the British government. Thus, if there is a world slump, Britain's exports are bound to fall very substantially because of the fall in foreign purchasing power. Again, if the terms of trade move very substantially against Britain, that is, if import prices rise much more than export prices, then Britain needs to export much more to pay for the same quantity of imports. Events of this kind can have a very unfavourable effect on the British balance of payments, and the British government can do almost nothing to prevent them. On the other hand, there remains a great deal a Liberal government could do to improve the British balance-of-payments position, and to prevent some of the kinds of crises which have occurred since the war.

In the first place, by putting an end to inflation a Liberal government would prevent British export prices from rising in the way they have done almost continually since the war. If the export prices of one country rise more than the export prices of her competitors, her exports are bound to suffer, and the British price level has risen more than the price levels of Germany and the USA almost continuously since the war.[1] The post-war inflation has certainly harmed the British balance of payments, and a Liberal government could improve them by ending inflation.

[1] It was argued above that this was partly due to the fact that Germany and the USA have on the whole had more unemployment than Britain, but inflation needs to be stopped in Britain, even though this is more difficult to achieve than it is in some other countries.

In the second place, by using a more effective policy to control the level of demand, a Liberal government could prevent the kind of balance of payments crisis which occurred in 1955, which was mainly due to the fact that British manufacturers and consumers tried to use up far more goods than the economy could supply, with the result that much of the difference came from other countries with serious consequences for the balance of payments. By controlling the level of demand effectively, a Liberal government could prevent a crisis of this nature from occurring again.

On the more positive side, a Liberal government could do a number of things which would help Britain's export position. Through the Liberal government's policy to protect the British consumer, the quality and reliability of British exports would necessarily be improved. Some British goods have been criticized recently for their unreliability. In Britain many manufacturers issue guarantees which oblige a purchaser to sign away such legal guarantees as he has, and in addition to agree that the manufacturer's decision is binding in any dispute about the manufacturer's guarantee. Thus a manufacturer who issues a guarantee of this kind is under no legal obligation whatsoever to replace a defective part or article. When manufacturers of certain makes of motor-cars do replace defective parts, the labour cost of the replacement, which is often very substantial, is charged to the consumer. Articles in the Consumers Association's publication *Which?* have revealed that a number of products are bought in the British home market which are inferior in many respects to other products which are available at lower prices. This can only be because the consumer is ignorant of the real merits and the defects of the products available, and this ignorance is very largely due to the fact that much of the advertising that producers now pay for is not only uninformative, but often positively deceptive. The result of this is that producers do not necessarily need a high quality product if they are to sell well in Britain, and they do not necessarily need to produce reliable goods either. They merely need good advertising. In consequence many British goods are difficult to sell in other countries where standards are more rigorous, and where they have to compete more with high quality foreign manufactured goods. By protecting the British consumer from shoddy products, deceptive advertising, and inadequate guarantees, a Liberal government would do a great deal to improve the quality of British goods in export markets, and so Britain's export position would be improved. An improvement in the quality and reliability of British manufactured goods will be particularly important if we join the European Common Market. Our imports of manufactured goods will increase substantially if we join, and we shall need to increase our exports by an equivalent amount.

The policy a Liberal government could follow would improve the British balance of payments in three ways. British exports would be less likely to be priced out of world markets because of inflation in Britain, there would no longer be crises due to sudden bursts of excess demand, and the quality of British products would be improved, which would make them easier to sell abroad. These improvements would not necessarily prevent the occurrence of occasional crises, because developments in the rest of the world might create problems the British government had to deal with. If such problems arose, a Liberal government could deal with them in the following ways.

In the first place, it could do everything possible to strengthen international organizations like the International Monetary Fund, so that temporary crises could be dealt with by increasing British currency reserves through using British drawing rights on the International Monetary Fund, and by using up these currency reserves (which is after all the purpose of the reserves) rather than by pursuing a 'beggar my neighbour' policy of raising tariffs or introducing import restrictions. In the second place, where this is impossible, it could pursue a policy of making special tax concessions to exporters when more exports were needed. This would have the advantage that consumers' interests would not be damaged by import controls and tariffs which prevent consumers from buying some goods and cause them to pay very high prices for other goods. In this way a Liberal government's economic policy could ensure that balance-of-payment crises very rarely occurred, and that when they did occur, government policy would improve the balance of payments without restricting the freedom of choice of the consumer.

Since the war, Labour governments and Conservative governments have failed to prevent the recurrence of balance-of-payments crises. This has created the impression in the world that there is something wrong with the British economy. Britain has one of the highest standards of living in the world, the British economy is one of the most productive economies in the world, and it is absurd that it should be widely thought that the British economy is 'in a bad way'. By reducing balance-of-payments crises to a minimum, a Liberal government would end the legend of the weak British economy.

AVOIDING EXCESSIVE GOVERNMENT INTERFERENCE

A proliferation of controls and interferences in people's lives is one of the worst disasters that can afflict the people of a country. When an economy cannot be run without the rationing of food and clothing, the direction of labour, the need to get licences for all building, and the control of most employment by government ministries, then people's lives are being interfered with in important ways due to an economic failure. To produce the amount that the British people produce, in such a small country and in such a complicated way, a great deal of organization is obviously necessary. This organization can be obtained either by a set of people telling everybody what to do, and using the force of law to make them do it, or through the money mechanism. When the money mechanism is used, people are not ordered about by other people, but they change jobs in response to higher incomes which are offered in their new jobs, they are dissuaded from buying goods which are in short supply because such goods become expensive, they refrain from building when they cannot afford to build, and they employ as many people as they can afford to employ. The money mechanism is in fact doing the organizing which needs to be done. This has a number of advantages over a system where people do the organizing. In the first place, even if a set of planners could in theory organize the economy as well as the money mechanism, the people who would actually administer the plan would have failings which are all too well known by those who remember the bureaucracy in this country in the period of the post-war Labour governments. People often misuse their power, so it is desirable that the power of government officials to interfere in people's lives should be kept to a minimum.[1]

---

[1] See Dostoievski, *Letters from the Underworld*, bk. 1 for a fundamental indictment of the bureaucratic mentality.

In the second place, even if ideal bureaucrats could be found, it is likely that people on the whole prefer to have their decisions determined by impersonal forces rather than by other people. They then have the illusion that they can do whatever they please, even if many of their decisions are actually determined by economic factors. In the third place, it is widely felt that there are great political dangers in giving too much power to the central government of a country. For these reasons, a Liberal government would use the market mechanism as much as possible to achieve its economic aims. The market mechanism does not produce very good results if it is not interfered with at all, as the unemployment of 1920-39 shows, but the ideal is to try to make the economy work well, while keeping the interference with the market mechanism to a minimum. It is always possible to solve the problem of unemployment by ordering everybody to work, and telling them where to work, or to solve the problem of inflation by sending shopkeepers to prison if they raise their prices, or a balance-of-payments problem by refusing to allow people to buy foreign goods. A Liberal government would always try to solve economic problems by discovering lines of policy which restrict the interference of the government in people's lives to a minimum. There would be no danger that a Liberal government would ever afflict the British people with the disaster of regimented economy.

CONCLUSION

The Liberals are the only party which could provide a government to protect the British people from unemployment, inflation, frequent balance-of-payments crises, and the proliferation of controls. The Conservatives cannot provide a government which can protect the British people from inflation and balance-of-payments crises. Labour cannot provide a government which would protect the British people from a mass of controls and interferences, because it believes in planning for its own sake, and perhaps still believes in nationalization as well. In any case, the Labour Party has provided governments in the past which have completely failed to prevent inflation.

The economic policy which has been outlined so far has the aim of protecting the British people from certain kinds of economic disaster, and a Liberal government should give the very highest priority to these objectives. Within the limits of a policy which maintained continuous full employment and price stability together with a sound balance of payments and a freedom from government interference, a Liberal government would be free to pursue certain other economic aims, but the pursuit of these aims should never conflict with the fundamental policy which has been outlined.

Two positive aims of Liberal economic policy will now be outlined. These are, to protect the consumer's interests and to raise Britain's rate of economic growth.

HELPING THE CONSUMER

In the interests of the consumer, a number of reforms are urgently needed. These are:

1. *Banning Resale Price Maintenance*

In the United States, it is possible to buy gramophone records, cars, refrigerators, television sets, and most other consumer goods at up to 30% below the price the manufacturer suggests his goods should be sold at. If a motor-car salesman tried to sell most makes of car in this country at a price below the manufacturers' fixed retail price, he would be refused further supplies of cars, and he would be driven out of business. This is because individual resale price maintenance is permitted[1] in this country while it is illegal in most of the USA. Thus in this country shopkeepers are not allowed to cut many prices. This is clearly a case where the interests of the British people as consumers are sacrificed to give shopkeepers and businessmen a quiet life. The abolition of resale price maintenance is an urgently needed reform which would reduce the cost of living and stimulate competition.

2. *Improving the information which is available to consumers about the goods they buy*

Much of present-day advertising is deceptive. ITV should give up time to independent organizations who would test goods, and explain the real merits of the goods they have tested to viewers. A Liberal government could make it compulsory for all businesses who wished to advertise their products to submit the same products for independent and objective testing. In this way the

---

[1] It is even enforceable by law.

quality of many of the goods produced in Britain would be improved, because businessmen would no longer be able to pretend that their goods were better than they really were. As was argued above, this would also improve Britain's export performance. This is not done now because the Conservative government which set up ITV in its present form has always attached more importance to the interests of advertising firms than to the interests of the consumer.

3. Giving consumers legal guarantees for the quality of the goods they buy
A Liberal government could pass legislation which would oblige a business to replace any parts of a good which did not maintain the standard of performance which was claimed for them when the good was sold, over a period of, for instance, one year. Such replacement would need to be completely free. This would oblige businesses to improve the quality and reliability of their goods, which would also have a beneficial effect in export markets.

4. Protecting the consumer from inefficiency in the nationalized industries and the bureaucracy
A Liberal government could set up independent tribunals (ombudsmen) to whom people could bring complaints of inefficiency, ineptitude, and injustice on the part of the bureaucracy and the nationalized industries. These tribunals could have the power to recommend the fining or dismissal of the officials concerned. At present, people are not protected from the bureaucracy because Labour and Conservative governments have given a higher priority to featherbedding the bureaucrat than they have to the protection of the British people from bureaucratic inefficiency, complacency, and even sometimes downright maliciousness.

In these ways a Liberal government could do much to protect the interests of the consumer.

RAISING BRITAIN'S RATE OF GROWTH
We can only raise the rate of growth of a country which has continuous full employment and a labour force of constant size by continuously raising the productivity of that labour force. The main way in which this can be done is through continually improving the quality and quantity of machinery which workers use in production. If the rate of growth of a country without spare

7

labour, like Britain, is to be permanently raised, the emphasis must lie with the quality rather than the quantity of machinery. Simply increasing the quantity of machinery each worker works, without a continuous technical improvement in the productivity of that machinery, must eventually result in diminishing returns, because there is a limit to the amount of machinery a worker can effectively operate. It is however likely that at present we are some way from this limit, and increasing the rate of investment would probably substantially increase Britain's rate of economic growth for a number of years. In the normal way investment cannot be increased unless there is a reduction in consumption, but a substantial increase in the rate of investment in manufacturing industry at the expense of the nationalized industries would be possible in Britain if investments in the nationalized industries were only made when their yield was sufficient. The railway modernization programme, for instance, was to cost £1,500 million, and it was hoped (making the most optimistic possible assumptions, such as that new diesel trains will have a life of forty years) that its yield would be £85 million a year. It is thus hoped that this investment of £1,500 million will yield $5\frac{2}{3}\%$. At the same time, investment plans in manufacturing industry which were expected to yield 10–20% were being cut as a direct result of government policy. The investment which was being cut in manufacturing industry was mainly designed to serve expanding markets, and it was thus reasonably safe. The investment in the railways is in an industry with a declining market, and moreover a market which will decline much more as the people who do not own their own cars become fewer, and as fares fall and long distance traffic is diverted from rail to air. For these reasons investment in the railways would only be justified if its yield was expected to be at least 15–20%, in view of the risk involved. It is only on these terms that a businessman would dream of putting money into the railways. To permit investment in the railways when it is only expected to yield $5\frac{2}{3}\%$ is a waste of national resources, and it has the direct consequence of taking capital away from industries which would make much better use of it. Cutting out all investment by the nationalized industries which is insufficiently profitable would allow investment by manufacturing industry to be increased by a considerable amount, and this would temporarily raise Britain's rate of economic growth. Anyone who agrees with

Mr Wiles's argument in Part 2 about the immediate priority that should be attached to the achievement of a very high rate of economic growth will wish to increase investment by a greater amount than these suggestions would permit. Consumption would then need to be reduced to allow further increases in investment. If a Liberal government wished permanently to raise the rate of growth, it would need to make changes in the economy, which would result in a greater rate of increase in the productivity of new machinery which was installed in the economy. To do this, more improvements in machinery and production methods would need to be developed in the British economy, and improvements which were invented and developed abroad would need to be more rapidly introduced in Britain than they are at present. A Liberal government could take the following steps to ensure this:

1. *Increase in research and development in British industry*

In 1955–6, out of £300 million spent on research and development in Britain, £177 million, or 59%, was financed by the government as part of the 'defence' programme.[1] Much of this expenditure will have gone towards the independent British nuclear deterrent, which it is Liberal policy to abandon, and to other prestige ventures which a Liberal government would certainly look at very critically. This type of expenditure is damaging to the economy, mainly because the scientists and engineers who are employed on these projects would make very valuable contributions to the economy in other industries which are badly in need of them. The kind of research which is most needed is into improved methods of production and into the development of improved products in industries which produce consumer goods or machinery. Such improvements are responsible for economic growth, and they are also helpful to our balance-of-payments position. It is often argued that research into defence and 'prestige' projects is helpful to the economy, because discoveries are often made which have applications which can be used in ordinary economic activity. The weakness in this argument is that, while it is obviously true that any increase in knowledge is likely to have some economic applications eventually, research activity

---

[1] *DSIR Survey on Research and Development in British Manufacturing Industry in 1955*, Cmd 902, HMSO 1958.

which has commercial applications in mind will produce more economically usable results faster.

From the point of view of achieving a fast rate of growth, it it particularly important that large research and development expenditures should be made in the industries which produce machinery, because a continuous improvement in the productivity of new machinery leads to higher productivity wherever that machinery is installed.[1] The benefit to the economy from improved machinery is much greater than the benefit which is likely to accrue to the firms which produce it.[2] There is a case here for using public funds to finance research and development by the machinery producing industries.

It is notable that in 1957 the Russians employed 2,450 people on machine-tool research and development in one organization (ENIMS), while our industry employed about 1,750 people on research and development in 123 different firms. The Russians may have resources in their large research organization which none of our 123 firms can match, and the result may be faster improvements in Russian machinery. On the other hand a Russian novelist[3] has suggested that the concentration of research into large organizations brings all the disadvantages of bureaucratic control with it. The relative efficiency of a few large research associations, or a large number of small ones, is something which it is important for us to know about. It is certain that without government support we shall never have research associations as large as ENIMS in this industry, and if this very large type of research association proves to be more effective, that alone would be sufficient to give the Russian economy a permanently higher rate of growth.

2. *Improvements in education*

Even in purely economic terms, money spent on university

---

[1] An increase in productivity by the machinery which produces machinery leads to a cheapening of machinery throughout the economy, so there is a benefit throughout the whole of manufacturing industry when there is an increase of productivity in this one industry. It is significant that the Russians use automation to make machinery to a much greater extent than any Western economy.

[2] The gain is shared between the firms which produce the superior machinery, the firms which use it, the workers who work it who may get higher wages, and the consumer who may be able to buy goods at lower prices. Even if the machinery producer has monopoly power (through patents, for instance), it will pay him to pass on part of the gain.

[3] Dudintsev, *Not by Bread Alone* (1957).

expansion has a high yield, because it eventually permits industries which need a large number of scientists and engineers to expand relatively to industries which require fewer skills. In the past century there has been a pronounced increase in the share of world markets going to industries which need scientists and engineers, and this trend is likely to continue. It is certainly in our economic interests to employ a higher proportion of our labour force in this kind of industry.

A Liberal government could also found more technical colleges and subsidize apprentice training schemes within firms. The case for subsidizing apprentice training schemes is that the gain to the economy from the training of apprentices is much greater than the gain to the firms which train them, since the firms lose a high proportion of their apprentices once they are trained. Firms must then train much fewer than the optimum number from the point of view of the economy as a whole. A Liberal government should also give financial help to any workers who took courses in night schools and technical colleges.

3. *Action against monopoly*

A Liberal government could speed up the rate at which foreign scientific and technological developments are introduced in the British economy by making British industry more competitive through stiffer legislation against monopolistic and restrictive practices. It could improve the ability of the economy to absorb foreign production methods by founding institutions like the Harvard Business School to educate British managerial staff in modern management methods.

These reforms, by raising Britain's rate of technical advance, would certainly help to raise our rate of economic growth.

This chapter has tried to show how a Liberal government could maintain full employment, stable prices, a sound balance of payments, a higher rate of economic growth, and a better deal for the consumer. And only a Liberal government could carry out this policy – other parties are too committed to the interests of pressure groups within the economy.

PART FOUR

A Programme for Education

A. D. C. PETERSON

A Liberal policy for education must be true to the two main principles for which this party and, it now seems, this party alone has always stood in Britain: it must be prepared to be radical and its aim must be freedom. Radical, because education is an issue of the greatest national importance, and if changes are required, changes must be made, however uncomfortable the process. There is nothing that matters more to most of us as individuals, or to all of us as a people, than how our children are educated. To neglect this is individual selfishness and national suicide. Most people of all parties would agree to this. For years we have spent far too much of our national income on wasteful or useless defence projects or on the maintenance of a so-called 'prestige' which looks back to the nineteenth century. In the last few years we have just begun to realize that the future lies with the highly educated nations and to step up the proportion of our investment in our children.

But it is not enough to begin to realize – and we are not doing more than that – the importance of education. As well as spending more, we must be prepared to think about it and, if need be, break and remould some of our accepted patterns. In a society which is changing more rapidly than ever before, we cannot afford an educational system which is either immune to change or so intricately governed by checks and balances that change in education necessarily follows far behind change in the economic and social structure for which the children are educated. There must be at least the possibility of rapid and radical adaptation. Equally, for a Liberal the objective of such a radical approach to the educational system must surely be the extension of human freedom. It will be the main purpose of this essay to suggest a radical re-examination of restrictions on freedom in education. In doing so we must be very clear whose freedom we are talking about. Is it the teacher's? Or the child's? Or the family's? Or the local authority's?

There is one common misconception that possibly needs to be cleared up in advance. It is often said that it would be better if we could keep education out of politics altogether. This view is perhaps unusually common today because, in the controversy over the comprehensive school, both Conservative and Labour supporters have suspected that the opposing party is not genuinely concerned with educational issues at all, but is surreptitiously trying to use a particular form of school organization to secure a purely political advantage. To make support for a particular educational theory, as opposed to an educational system, a test of party orthodoxy is to fall into the Lysenko fallacy. But this is a very different thing from wanting to 'keep education out of politics'. Those who want to keep their own sphere of interest out of politics are usually trying to avoid the possibility of democratic control or discussion, so that they may either maintain a 'hallowed' system or impose control by experts. And by experts they mean themselves and their friends. As a result things that are 'taken out of politics' have a habit of stagnating and falling into the hands of those with a natural interest in preserving the *status quo*. The true situation can be seen quite clearly if we take the parallel case of medicine. No one would, in a free society, suggest that different treatments of arthritis should become a political issue, any more than different methods of teaching French. At the same time we would all now surely agree that the system adopted for securing the health of the nation is a legitimate and national political issue: and I believe that we should now accept the same status for the educational system. If, then, there are avoidable restrictions on human freedom in our present educational system, or built-in restraints which prevent it from adapting itself with sufficient speed and flexibility to a changing world, it is by political means that we must seek to remove them.

If one tries to ·look at the English educational system with a fresh eye, one cannot help being struck by the extent of restriction, selection, and specialization. Again and again, during the school and university career, the individual child or youth is tested, graded, allocated, examined, forced to compete for entry to the next stage, or to make irrevocable choices between incompatible alternatives. It is difficult for people in this country to realize that throughout most of Europe children are not graded into 'bright' and 'dull' streams in primary schools; do not face a critical selection test between the ages of 10 and 11; do not choose between a literary and a scientific education between 15 and 16 or even earlier; and do not have to compete with their contemporaries for a strictly limited number of university places. It is worth considering how far these peculiarities of the English system are the result of a deliberate educational or socio-political theory; and how far they are the half accidental outcome of a self-regulating traditional system. And we must surely question more radically than we have yet done how far they are tolerable to those who respect the traditional liberal values. These values, I suggest, are still to be found in the aims of the French Revolution: Liberty, Equality, and Fraternity. It is not the truth of these concepts but their compatibility in practice that we have subsequently questioned, just as we have recognized the dangers of exalting any one over the other two as a supreme value. Nevertheless, no system of education which does not seek all three, to the greatest extent to which they can be harmonized, is genuinely liberal.

If we look at the 'tripartite' organization of secondary education as initially implemented in England and Wales it seems, for all its good intentions, to have offended in practice against all three. Liberty was clearly restricted when the choice of secondary school was put firmly in the hands of the local education authority. Previously the middle-class family could and frequently did choose a grammar school education for the children, through payment of a very modest fee. The abolition of fees and the transfer to the local education authority of the vital choice was clearly based on the belief that the authority, guided by expert techniques of selection, would prove able to decide better than child or parent which school the child should go to. For the next ten years educational research in England was concentrated on this question of selection for secondary education, in the hope of producing a selection technique which could live up to this fearful responsibility. Whether one believes that the search has been successful or not depends upon the level of social injustice that one is prepared to tolerate. Allowing for a small proportion of exceptional cases (which includes those rich enough to be educated privately) the decision is probably the most important in the life history of any Englishman today. On his performance in the tests, usually administered between his tenth and eleventh birthday, depends his lifelong status as a member of the professional and managerial, or labouring and technical, classes. The best educational opinion seems to agree that we can never hope to reach a degree of accuracy which will mean less than one child in twenty wrongly allocated. If this one in twenty were my own child, I should regard this an as unacceptable interference by the State with my, and his, liberty: and this seems to have been the general reaction of the English people. I should prefer in any case to have more say in my child's education; but to surrender this to an outside authority which makes decisions vitally affecting his whole life when he is 10 years old, and makes them wrong once in twenty, is too much. Hence, perhaps, the flourishing condition of the 'private sector' of education.

Control of selection is of course the greatest encroachment on liberty, but there are many others: authorities which will not allow children to cross their 'frontier' in order to attend a more convenient or a preferred school, authorities which frown on co-education or impose it, authorities who will help with boarding fees inside their frontiers but not beyond. In all sorts of respects the local education authority infringes more than is necessary upon the freedom of the individual. Of course no authority can provide parents with all the variety of choice they would like, but too often it is the authority's conviction that it 'knows best' rather than the physical circumstances that limit the parents' choice.

Equality has suffered no less. Socialism we are told 'is about equality'. This is or should be far truer of Liberalism than it is of Socialism, which is really about the State control of our economic life. No Liberal can see the division of the people into 'two nations' by the 'eleven-plus' and the 'rise of the meritocracy'[1] without misgivings. One of the strongest arguments in favour of the comprehensive school is that it is designed to preserve a sense of social unity between future 'managers' and 'men' which the tripartite system goes out of its way to destroy: one of the most telling but certainly not established arguments against it is that it may fail in this task almost as badly as its rival. The threat to equality has been perhaps an even stronger factor in public rejection of the original eleven-plus selection than the threat to liberty.

And what has happened to fraternity? There are two senses in which we can use this ideal as a measuring stick of educational systems. The first, and clearly the most important one, is very close to 'equality'. Of course there is intellectual inequality in any

---

[1] Cf. Michael Young, *The Rise of the Meritocracy* (1958).

society; and of course intellectual unequals require different forms of education. It is possible, as the Americans have found, to be so impressed by the importance of equality that the liberty of the abler child or youth to develop his own talents is unduly restricted. But a system which by a process of segregation actually increases the gap between intellectual unequals is illiberal and sins against fraternity. Men should, as brothers, be concerned to help and not continually to surpass each other. An educational system which starts streaming and competition for further advancement at the age of 8 (for the eleven-plus, like the eighteen-plus, is in fact competitive, whatever it may be in theory) is not furthering the brotherhood of man.

But there is a second and more limited meaning of fraternity which is relevant to this whole selection process. Segregation at eleven-plus treats the child as if he or she were a single, measurable entity and not, as he is in fact, a living and growing member of a family. How many of the 'grammar school failures' are children who were allocated to an academic education as a result of tests carried out on their 'native intelligence', but without reference to the wishes or 'support' of their families? How many of the small band of 'late developers', who fight their way back from an initial rejection, are those whose wit was a fraction slow at the age of 10, but who have the support and encouragement of a family with intellectual interests? And how many children frustrate the unfraternal intentions of the authority by deliberately 'failing the eleven-plus' in order to go to the same school as their brothers, sisters, or friends?

The age at which a child breaks the close family tie and becomes an individual, to be treated by the State as an individual, varies of course, but it is surely much later than 10. Perhaps a good number of those apparently intelligent children, who became 'grammar school failures' because they were wrenched from the cultural background of their home at the age of 11, might have developed their full intellectual ability a little later, of their own free choice, if they had been allowed to defer the decision.

THE TWO-TIER SOLUTION

It is not surprising, therefore, that a strong body of opinion, both among the general public and among those particularly concerned with education, has turned against the whole concept of a major segregation among children at the age of 11. The main alternatives are of course the comprehensive school and some form of 'two-tier education'. The first means that all secondary education is concentrated in the same school, although an elaborate system of 'sets' and 'classes' allows each to progress at his or her own pace in the different academic subjects. This frees the comprehensive school from the accusation of retarding the able, as at one time the American High School undoubtedly did, only to open it to the charge (by no means proved) that internal streaming leads to a segregation even more bitter and unfraternal, because more obvious, than streaming into different schools. Two-tier education means basically postponing the decision for a more prolonged academic education to the age of 13 or 14, and inserting a common period of secondary education as a preliminary. Incidentally, under one two-tier system at least – the Leicestershire plan – the decision at 14 is left to be made not by the authority but by the parents. Both alternatives claim the advantage that they free the primary school from the pressure of 'preparing for the eleven-plus', which undoubtedly has a restrictive effect upon primary school teaching today. Two-tier systems have the great advantage that they *could* be put into operation throughout the whole country comparatively quickly, using existing buildings. That a national system of comprehensive schools is not a practical possibility has been adequately shown by Dr Robin Pedley. The majority of existing secondary schools are too small, and built on too constricted sites, for adaptation as comprehensives, and no government could really consider scrapping these and building a complete new secondary system.

There is, however, one new factor which has arisen since Dr Pedley's survey and which may significantly alter the picture it presented. This is the explosive increase in the size of sixth forms – 20% in the three years between 1958 and 1960. Since the minimum size of a comprehensive school was originally determined by the number of pupils required to produce a sixth form of adequate size, this dramatic increase in the proportion of each 'grammar stream' staying on to the sixth form may mean that we can reduce the minimum size of the comprehensive school. And this, in turn, may mean that many sites and buildings which were rejected as being too small for conversion into comprehensives could be reconsidered.

It is probably too soon to come to any conclusion about the best modifications or alternatives to segregation. I cannot help wishing, however, that there had been as much experiment in providing non-academic courses within the grammar school for the wrongly allocated as in providing GCE courses within the secondary modern.

On the other hand, we have by now had enough experience of straight segregation to be sure that it is not the Liberal answer, and it should surely be Liberal policy to use the powers of the Ministry of Education to reinforce the movement that has already begun. If it would be too soon to recommend any particular solution (and no one solution might ever be appropriate for all areas) the Minister could and should require local authorities to satisfy him that they were taking all reasonable steps to eliminate irrevocable segregation at 11. And it would not be a sufficient reply for them to point to the meagre possibilities of transfer between radically differentiated schools.

THE PUBLIC SCHOOLS

Another form of segregation by schools which troubles not only the Liberal conscience but all who are concerned with education is the position of the public schools and the private preparatory schools. No Liberal, I imagine, would seriously contemplate rigid legislation to 'abolish' these schools. Apart from the natural reluctance to forbid all education outside the State system, a measure of tyranny unparalleled in education west of the iron curtain, the political imbecility of denying to the churches the right to provide education is hardly conceivable. And in any case many public schools would probably migrate, and rightly migrate, to Eire. At the same time it is pretty clear that the extent of the breach between the maintained system and the independent system in England is a misfortune. It *does* mean an accentuation of class consciousness which is deplorable and, however much public school headmasters may deplore it, it *is* true that many parents buy a public school education for their children, not because it is a better education (which it usually, but not always, is), but because they think it will give them a class and economic advantage. This may be an unpleasant fact, but it is a fact. And, what is more, these parents are right. A public school education does at present confer these advantages. But this is not the only sense in which the uniquely leading position occupied by our private schools is a misfortune. It means that by and large the children of the governing class are educated outside the national system: so that the members of the governing class do not know from personal experience where the educational shoe pinches. Honourable and public-spirited men in all parties are of course concerned about classes of fifty, earth closets and school buildings condemned fifty years ago: but it is difficult to imagine that they would not be more concerned if their own children were attending them. In most western countries which have no such widely developed and admirably conducted 'private sectors', they would be. Let us admit, then, that we have inherited, largely through our own refusal to contemplate, in the nineteenth century, a national system of secondary education, a social breach which is an historical misfortune. It has given us some of the finest schools in Europe, but it has helped to divide the nation and it has taken the edge off the desire for educational improvement. Is there any way in which the breach can be narrowed? On the whole the governors and headmasters of the public schools are as anxious as anyone to narrow it, but all proposals to reserve a proportion of public school places for pupils selected by local authorities have broken down on the question of selection. Boarding education at a public school is often better, and always more expensive, than boarding education at a local grammar school; and boarding education at secondary modern schools is unfortunately almost non-existent. Public schools say they will be glad to take pupils from maintained schools. But by what criterion can a local education authority justify spending the additional proportion of the ratepayers' money required to take up a place offered at Eton for John Smith, when it sends his neighbour Tom Brown to its own school round the corner? It is not a question of selecting the most intelligent, for this would turn the public schools into intellectual hot-houses and deprive the grammar schools of their most promising pupils. It is not a question of selecting the 'problem children' (beyond a very small percentage) because this would turn the public schools into 'special' schools, drive away their 'private' pupils and ultimately deprive problem children of the very atmosphere of normality which was being sought for them. It is not a question of selecting the child whose home circumstances make boarding desirable, because boarding can be provided much more cheaply and without any special privilege at maintained grammar schools.

The future of the public schools presents, then, one of the toughest problems in English education, but one that will not be solved by leaving it alone and sitting on the safety-valve. Whatever solution Liberals are to work for it should, if possible, be one which public schools will be ready to adopt voluntarily, and one which will allow them to preserve their corporate identity. The following plan is tentatively suggested on the assumption that the public schools are themselves genuinely anxious to seek closer integration into the national pattern of education and to diminish their class isolation. First, let them offer a third of their places free of tuition fees and with boarding costs reduced to the same scale as those in maintained grammar schools. To offer less than a third would not significantly alter their class structure. Since many of them were, in their origins, charitable foundations and are supported by charitable endowments, the first contribution to the cost might well come from such funds. It is surely a questionable use of charitable endowments to devote them to reducing the cost of an upper-class education to those already better off than most. But the whole cost could not come from such sources. Would it not be a reasonable exchange that, whenever a public school was prepared to do this, the government should contribute for each pupil – and not merely for each free pupil – a sum equivalent to the present cost per head of secondary education? The school would then have entered the national system and could legiti-mately claim support from it. The main objection to the present direct-grant system would not hold, since there would be no 'creaming' of the best from the grammar schools. And since the free-placers would not be costing local authorities any more than other children, the problems of selection would be much easier and could be based upon the sheer need for boarding-places for the children of men employed in certain categories which involve travel – servicemen, bargees, or ministers of religion, for instance – and of widows. Grants toward the cost of boarding-fees would be made by local authorities on an income scale, just as they are now towards boarding fees at maintained grammar schools.

It might be that some public schools, perhaps mainly those with no charitable endowments, would not wish to enter such a scheme. For them there is another possible line of development.

8

They were founded largely to provide good secondary education at a time when the State could not, or would not, do so. It seems likely that over the next two or three decades there is going to be a large demand, which the State will not be able to meet, for 'college' education of a less specialized kind than the universities now provide, and perhaps at a lower age – say from 17 to 20. If a public school decided to move into this range of education, it would no longer be in competition with the maintained system. It would be providing an extra benefit for which it would seem reasonable that parents should pay. And it could reasonably expect local authorities to take up places at their own expense. In this way it might free itself from one of its increasing problems – the attempt to retain within schoolboy *mores* young people who, out of school, regard themselves, and are regarded by others, as adults.

If public schools were not prepared to adopt either of these patterns of change, or similar patterns of their own devising, then it would seem reasonable for the State to withdraw from them all privileges which they enjoy now as recognized partners in the national pattern of education. Such a policy might lead to a rise in the cost of public school education for fee-payers; and perhaps to the death of those public schools opposed to change. But there would be undoubted gains to the nation from such a loss. And many middle-class parents, who at present cripple themselves by school fees in order not to deprive their children of what they have come to think of as a birthright, might abandon the unequal struggle with relief so long as the Joneses abandoned it too.

But if negotiations of this kind with the public schools are to have any hope of success, they will have to be conducted by the Ministry of Education on a national level. The problem has proved too big for individual schools and individual local authorities. And it is clearly bound up with other possible reforms in the national pattern. Certainly if a change in our educational system, initiated from the centre, led to a wider adoption of 'two-tier' secondary education in the maintained system it would simplify the narrowing of the breach, since the 'break' in the maintained system would then come around the age of 13 or 14 as it does in the private system. In the long run, however, this breach will never be wholly closed until the maintained schools are actually as good as or better than the private ones. One can see this already by the growing prestige of some of the best maintained secondary schools and by the greater readiness of richer parents to use the maintained primary school where this is modern, well-staffed, and not overcrowded. Selection devices may get some of the children from poorer homes into the independent schools: only an improvement in standards will get children from richer homes into the maintained ones. And socially both movements are desirable. The second movement might well start at the beginning. Given adequate staff and modern buildings, English primary education is one of the things of which we can be justly proud. But this whole achievement is threatened by a growing shortage of teachers. Only if an expanded training college system concentrates almost entirely on the production of primary teachers can the objective of eliminating oversize classes by 1980 be achieved. This is no place to expatiate on the implications of this for the training college as an institution, or its chances of maintaining recruitment for purely primary training; but it does look as if the only hope of starting to bridge the gap at the bottom, by attracting the children of all classes into the maintained primary school, was by raising the age of *compulsory* education from 5 to 6, as recommended by the Liberal Education Advisory Committee in 1954 – perhaps using the extra flexibility provided to allow for more *voluntary* nursery schools. Such a change, coupled with the removal of eleven-plus pressure, might enable the primary schools to introduce on a wider scale modern languages, elementary science, and mathematics as opposed to arithmetic, and so to provide for their more gifted children a greater challenge than at present, while narrowing the gap between primary schools and preparatory schools.

THE CURRICULUM

The second great area where restriction, selection, and specialization operate against liberty, equality, and fraternity is in the content of education, the organization of the curriculum. In the primary stage this is not so marked, though the narrowness of the last two years of our primary curriculum is largely the result of pressure for the eleven-plus. How rarely do our 'primary' children start a foreign language before 11, for instance, as many Europeans and all privately educated English do. At the secondary stage however, competition for entry to universities, which is now beginning to be called pressure at eighteen-plus, has long had an acknowledged distorting effect and is going to be considerably more intense in 1965–6 than it is today. Many people shy away from the words 'curriculum' and 'syllabus'; a recent Minister of Education has referred to them as a 'secret garden'; yet if education matters, there can be few things in it that matter more than what is actually taught in the secondary schools. Who decides, in this country, what languages the next generation shall learn, the kind and amount of history and geography to be studied, the age at which a choice is to be imposed between abandoning either mathematics or literature? The naïve answer would be that, in our extremely anarchic system, neither the local education authority nor the Ministry of Education interferes in such matters; the headmaster of each school is free to decide for himself. Nothing could be further from the truth. If it were true, you would expect to find a wide divergence between the programmes of different secondary schools, in accordance with the differing views of their headmasters: in fact the programmes of all grammar schools and of the GCE streams of comprehensive and secondary modern schools are singularly alike – and singularly like what they were fifty years ago.[1] 83% of all GCE ordinary level passes in modern languages are in French, 13% in German, 3% in Spanish and 0·3% in Russian. It is hardly possible to maintain that such a distribution represents either the free choice of the pupils or the considered view of the headmasters about the relative value of the four languages. Other European countries during the twentieth century have changed the first or second foreign language taught in their schools, in accordance with the changing importance of these languages. England has no freedom to bring about such a change. A fluent speaking and reading knowledge of French has of course a great cultural and 'touristic' value. Yet how few 'O' level candidates acquire it. And for those who continue their languages further for vocational reasons, the McMeeking report indicates that for commercial purposes the order of priority is German, Spanish, Portuguese, French, while scientists are agreed that for their purpose it is German and Russian almost equally.

The secondary school curriculum in England is in fact controlled, and very rigidly controlled, by two widely dispersed

[1] Cf. J. A. Petch, *Fifty Years of Examining* (1953), p. 83.

forces, neither of which is susceptible to argument, or even fully conscious that it is exercising the control. The first is the sheer force of inertia, the tendency of teachers, unless stimulated by some outside pressure, to repeat in their teaching what they were taught themselves. This largely accounts for the myriads of boys and girls learning French who would rather – and rightly rather – be learning German, Spanish, or Russian; or for 'historians' repeating the Tudors and Stuarts for a second time rather than studying the evolution of the British Commonwealth. The only remedy for this is that someone at some stage should be given the right to apply the outside pressure or inducement. The disease in its classic form is almost certainly more prevalent in England and Wales than elsewhere, because there and there alone university graduates are permitted to return direct from the university to the schools, to undertake a lifetime of teaching their 'subject', without any professional training whatever. Some no doubt interest themselves in the problems of their profession and learn from experience, but the temptation to teach that area of the subject which one was taught oneself, and in the way in which one was taught oneself, must be very strong. What other model has the untrained graduate to work on? This, then, is surely a case where the freedom of the teacher to teach how and what he likes must be limited in the interests of the pupil. The very least that society has a right to ensure is that the teacher should be made aware that there are other methods and other periods than those which his own teacher chose, and that there should be some authority which has the power and the will to stimulate, and in the very last resort enforce, a change in the curriculum, whether it is the substitution of a new language for an old, or the introduction of some newly developed branch of mathematics. The authority through which society must act to effect this is surely the State, the Ministry of Education, and not a local authority. As a first step, it should be Liberal policy to bring England and Wales into line with all other European countries and make professional training compulsory for graduates who propose to become professional teachers. This is the more important since an increasing proportion of them will soon be teaching in secondary modern schools. It is in any case the recommendation of the National Advisory Council and it should be our policy as Liberals to see that it is put into effect.

ENTRANCE TO THE UNIVERSITIES

The second force which controls the curriculum of secondary schools is the entrance requirements of the universities, as expressed in terms of the GCE. Although rather less than half our sixth forms are in fact preparing to enter universities, and not much more than half of grammar school pupils ever enter the sixth form at all, these entrance requirements do in fact govern the whole grammar school curriculum. In the sixth form it is probably right that they should do so. It is possible in large grammar schools to divide the sixth form into a 'pre-university' and a 'non-university' course, as is widely done in American comprehensive High Schools. But there are very sound arguments against it, and it would not be practicable in our smaller selective schools. What is perhaps less defensible is the extent to which syllabuses for GCE 'O' level are drawn up on the assumption that they represent Part I of a course in the subject leading to university entrance: so that these requirements push their controlling influence down into the early years of the grammar school course and the later stages of the secondary modern. Granted, however, that the requirements of university entrance and the final school leaving examination – which may or may not be the same thing – inevitably control in any system the last two years of secondary school work, it becomes all the more important to ensure that these examinations are themselves controlled, with the interests of the secondary school in mind and in such a way as to provide the maximum degree of freedom for pupils and teachers. The only limitations on this freedom should be the obligation to the pupils themselves and to their parents to give them a general and liberal education, and the obligation to the universities to give them sufficient academic grounding to fit them for their university course. These are the aims recognized throughout western civilization, but the procedure used to attain them varies. In all European countries other than England and Wales the pattern of the curriculum is laid down by the State: it is the degree of control over the syllabus in individual subjects which varies, and in this respect the extremes are found in France and Germany.

In France the syllabuses are prescribed in some detail by the State, but the pupil is given considerable freedom of choice through the existence of a variety of courses, biased either in one direction or another: in Germany the school is genuinely free to follow its own syllabus. The prescribed physics syllabus for a typical German *abitur* examination consists of ten lines, that of an English GCE 'A' level of 150. It is difficult to maintain that the English is the freer system. In England and Wales the refusal of the State to accept any responsibility for the content of secondary education has in fact left the power divided between a number of independent authorities, but certainly not in the hands of the teachers. The examinations themselves are set and corrected by nine different independent examining boards. It is sometimes held that, from the point of view of content and method, this itself provides for freedom and variety, since the school, if not the pupil, has nine different examinations to choose between. But this freedom is illusory. In the first place, some of the boards are already so overloaded that they cannot 'accept' new clients. More important is the fact that the examination must, in practice, be taken as a whole, and a geography teacher for instance, who prefers the type of paper set by the Cambridge Local, is quite unable to change over to that board if, as usually happens, his physics and mathematics colleagues have an equal preference for the 'styling' of the board with which they are already working. In practice the great majority of schools have therefore long settled down as clients of a particular board, and any freedom of choice is limited to the options offered by that board alone. From the point of view of content, therefore, any one pupil's main sixth form course will be controlled by the syllabus of whichever local examining board his school has enrolled with. A degree of freedom exists here, since the board itself is often quite as anxious to promote variety as the schools are to embrace it, and the syllabuses are kept under review by panels on which school-teachers are represented. It cannot be as great a degree of freedom, however, as under a national examination system, and it would be well to remember that the general experience of these panels as media for revising rather than adding to syllabuses has not been happy. As so often happens, a series of compromises is weighted in the direction of conservatism. It is a very normal pattern of development in this shrinking world that a number of comparatively small local bodies should coalesce either into a few regional ones or a single national one. The time has surely come for this to happen with the GCE. The Minister would be wise to leave the conduct of the examination in the hands of an autonomous body representing the schools, the universities, and public authority; but the case for making this a single national body, possibly with regional advisory councils, is now strong. The SSEC, it is true, dismisses the idea in its latest report.[1] In speaking of the difficulties of maintaining equivalent standards they say: 'We can think of nothing short of a scheme for conducting the examination through a single central body – a project not likely to command much support – which would eliminate it altogether.' But they have not, in any of their three reports, discussed what reasons would be brought forward against the single central body. The reasons in favour of it seem to be fourfold. First, it would give the schools, and even in large schools individual pupils, a much more genuine freedom of choice. Instead of nine different syllabuses, only one of which could be chosen, because the school was tied to a particular board, it might be possible for the national board to offer three or four alternative syllabuses in each subject all to be examined on the same day and any one of which could be combined with any one of the alternatives in other subjects. Second, it would make very much easier the maintenance of equivalent standards as the SSEC admit. Third, it would be some safeguard against the 'exhaustion of questions': particularly in the type of examination paper which really tests understanding rather than memory (e.g. the new special papers suggested by the SSEC) there is a limited number of really effective questions which can be asked. The more examination papers are set each year the more difficult it becomes for examiners to think of new and effective questions; and the habit of 'working old papers' as preparation for an examination makes old questions very dangerous. Apart from these positive advantages there is probably a considerable saving in costs and man-power to be achieved by rationalization. It is difficult not to conclude that such a national examination would also fit in better with the recommendation, now before the Minister, that a revised GCE 'A' and 'S' level should be accepted by all universities as a common entrance examination. The only *caveat* entered to this recommendation was in favour of the rights of the Oxford colleges to conduct their own entrance tests; and with the movement towards common papers even here, it seems not impossible that this also could be overcome, provided that

[1] *Third Report of the Secondary School Examinations Council*, HMSO (1960).

the new 'S' papers proved a success, and that the scripts, or photographic copies of them, could be sent to the colleges for individual assessment. What the colleges are concerned with is presumably their right to interview, assess, and select their own entrants, not a special claim to be expert in the setting of papers for sixth formers, with whose educational background the board would be much more familiar than the college entrance committee.

The final advantage to be derived from such a reorganization is that it would put responsibility for the secondary curriculum clearly on the shoulders of a single, identifiable body. It is right that university faculties and colleges should have wide discretion in selecting students for admission; it is unfortunately inevitable that as long as the shortage of university places continues, and even afterwards, there will be stiff competition for entry to certain faculties and universities; but the anarchic tangle of their individual preferences should not determine the curriculum of the secondary school. A general school leaving examination conducted under the control of a single national board could establish the general pattern of academic secondary education with all the opportunities of freedom and variety which are now denied to the schools. Where it imposed a particular requirement this would be done in the interests of national education after long discussion and careful consideration, not arbitrarily at the behest of some fractional interest. It would be in the last resort susceptible to public pressure, and its relations with the Ministry of Education might well be somewhat similar to those of the Bank of England with the Treasury.

If it is the nine examining boards who at present control the syllabus, it is the universities who control the pattern of the curriculum and the level of specialized knowledge required. Here anarchy reigns unchallenged. There is, of course, an agreed pattern and level laid down by the universities for their *entrance qualifications*. But in this country, unlike most others, to qualify for entrance to the university does not confer admission: to gain a university place the candidate must compete successfully for admission to the department, or, at Oxford and Cambridge, to the college. It is therefore the departments and the colleges who determine the pattern and the level required of the last two years of secondary school. In doing so they are a law to themselves and their main concern is not the effect which their selection methods may have on sixth form education but their very natural desire to secure in a chemistry faculty the best qualified chemist. A college may be concerned to admit a few 'good college men', but in the majority of cases the committee there too are looking for the men likely to do best in their final Honours Schools. It is not surprising therefore that the influence of these controlling factors on the sixth form curriculum is steadily in favour of more and more intense specialization, until schoolmasters complain that their pupils are expected to cover the first year of university work at school. As C. P. Snow has said: 'All the lessons of our educational history suggest we are only capable of increasing specialization, not decreasing it.' There is therefore at this crucial point a marked lack of freedom in the English educational system. It arises, as so often happens, not as the result of a calculated exercise of power, but of anarchy. The power is there, but it is exercised by people who hardly know that they possess it, and who are accountable to no one but themselves. The remedy is not to abolish the power. That would be impossible. The remedy is to bring the power under conscious, public, and accountable control. In other words, since the conditions of entry to the universities inevitably control the last two years' work in the grammar school, they cannot be left in the sole control of departmental or college entrance committees, whose legitimate claims would be met if they had the right to select the best qualified in their own fields, out of those who had completed a general secondary education controlled at a national level.

THE LOCAL AUTHORITIES

One recurring theme, rather surprising to the Liberal mind, seems to emerge from these detailed examinations of the restrictions on our educational freedom and threats to fraternity. It is the belief that the magnitude of the public need involved has got beyond the scope of the nexus of local authorities and autonomous bodies through whose hands the power is at present distributed. The rising cost of education alone, and its recognition as an issue of major national importance, has made the relationship of central and local authority a debated issue in all the English-speaking territories, where local control of education has been a long-standing tradition.

In England and Wales, education already accounts for the major part of the average local authority's budget. It is by far the most important issue still left in the hands of locally elected councils. And yet it would be difficult to maintain that these councils consist of people primarily interested in education, or who devote themselves primarily to educational matters. Nor are local elections commonly fought on educational issues. Indeed no elections are fought on educational issues, since national elections treat education as a local government matter, and local elections are now fought on national party lines. The whole administration of education may be suffering, in fact, from being the one major function remaining in the hands of bodies who were not primarily constituted for this purpose, and whose 'constituency boundaries' and political structure are no longer appropriate. Lancashire with a school population of 340,000 is a local education authority: so are Rutland with 3,300 and Eastbourne with 6,500. It is difficult to hold simultaneously that all are of the appropriate size.

The arguments usually brought forward in favour of local control of education, as opposed to regional or national, are three. All of them are superficially attractive to the Liberal mind. The first is that local control is a bulwark of freedom against the encroaching power of the State; the second is that local control allows for a greater freedom of experiment and flexibility within the system; the third is that local control stimulates local pride in local schools and therefore increased public support for educational expenditure. I very much doubt whether any of these arguments is now realistic. Incidentally, they could all have been put forward, had they been sufficiently sophisticated, by the feudal barons.

Local control as a bulwark of freedom depends primarily, of course, on the extent to which the local authority is in fact sensitive to the demands of local individuals. The freedom that matters is the freedom of individual parents, pupils, and teachers to give and seek the education that they think best; not the freedom of the Bottington County Borough Council to impose the kind of education it thinks best 'without interference from Whitehall'. Concern for this sort of freedom is likely to come, I suggest, either from men of genuine sensitivity to local needs and interest in educational affairs, or from men of wide and liberal education, not too intimately concerned with local issues. Control by *ad hoc* regional education boards, as suggested in the 1958 report of the Liberal Party Education Committee, would be more likely to produce the second type: does local government control still produce the first? It may have done so when local councillors were mostly residents of long standing, elected by fellow citizens of comparatively small areas, who had known them or known of them almost all their lives. Such a situation may well still exist in the small local authority like Rutland, but it is not the normal pattern. The far greater degree of mobility in the country today means that frequently neither councillors nor electors have lived very long in the same area, or that where men and women well advanced in years are elected, they are the representatives of a political party and quite unknown to the vast majority of their consituents. It is to the 'office' and not to the councillor that the perplexed parent turns for help or advice. On the other hand, the small local authority which may still command the goodwill, the deep local attachment, and the educational interest, too often suffers from a shortage of the financial means.

Moreover, existing local authorities suffer from the fact that few of their members stood for office because they were primarily interested in education. It may be objected that however true this may be of the county or borough council as a whole the 'real education authority' is the education committee, and this, through co-optation, does include many more members who genuinely represent the educational interest in the local community. This is a fallacy. The education committee is in fact advisory. Real power lies in the hands of the council as a whole and of other committees such as the finance committee. Indeed even in the education committee there is a practice already beginning of expecting that the co-opted members will abstain from voting on disputed issues. It would surely be worth careful consideration both by parents and teachers whether they would not be freer to seek their real educational aims if they found themselves face to face with the local officers of some kind of regional school board, representative perhaps of a group of local authorities, the Ministry and the teachers in the area, instead of to the County or Borough Council. As Mr John Vaizey has pointed out, such a system would also make it possible to introduce a larger element of professional self-government into the education service; and there is no reason to suppose that teachers would be any less free as employees of a regional board than they are as employees of a local authority.

The capacity of any educational system to evolve through experiment has always been important and is now more important than ever. It is clear that an extremely decentralized system like the English provides great opportunity for variety of experiment, provided that enough of the autonomous authorities are interested in experiment and have the resources to support it. The number of variations on the early methods of eleven-plus selection which have already been tried is evidence enough of this.

It is quite wrong, however, to suppose that systems with a stronger central control and larger regional units need be, or in fact are, backward in experiment. Two procedures can and do take the place of the spontaneous variety of experiment in England. The initiative may come from the Ministry of Education, which asks the teachers' associations to organize experiment along particular lines, providing of course the necessary material support, or the same process may work in reverse. Where experiment on a regional or school basis is required, the Ministry of Education can invite or instruct particular schools (like the *Lycées pilotes* in France) or particular regions to try out the new ideas. If education in England and Wales were a national system regionally organized, there is no reason whatever why the experiment and variety which we see among the 149 local education authorities should not be maintained. Indeed it might even be better supported and co-ordinated.

But it is not enough that experiment should take place. There must be adequate provision for the assessment and implementation of results. Here the centralized systems have all the advantage. I well remember a discussion with a group of Russian teachers who had just completed a three-months study-tour of the English educational system. 'Tell me,' was the first question, 'how do you ever change anything in your system? In Russia we may experiment for two or three years with a new development, but when we are satisfied that it is an improvement, the Ministry of Education will order its general adoption. What happens in your country?' The only possible reply was that, this country being a democracy, the necessary procedure was to persuade every one of a great number of free and autonomous authorities to move in the same direction simultaneously. Where this is a question of a change affecting one aspect of education only, this may prove a reasonable proposition; the spread of courses with a vocational bias in the secondary modern school is an example of an experimental success rapidly imitated all over the country; but where, as almost always happens, there are many interlocking interests, all of which must be persuaded to accept some modifications in their practice, the necessity of some central co-ordinating authority with power to impose final decisions becomes clearly apparent. One has only to look at the monotonous regularity with which first the Board, then the Ministry, and now the SSEC has been urging schools, universities, and examining boards to co-operate in lightening the load of specialist sixth-form work to see how slow the rate of change under this system of exhortation is – if indeed it moves at all. The SSEC report of 1960, for instance, merely reiterates the exhortation of the 1952 report. Eight years of discussion, experiment, and exhortation have left things rather worse than they were before.

Finally, how far is it true that local control and finance of education promotes pride in local schools and a readiness to find money for education? This theory has little support either from economists or from experience in this country. In theory revenue from rates is not likely to keep pace with a rising level of incomes, while revenue from taxes is. It is generally unsound, therefore, to argue that an expanding area of public service should be financed from rates, and to leave the expansion of educational expenditure to the local rates means no expansion. This was clearly recognized by the Association of Education Committees in their opposition to the substitution of block Treasury grants for the previous automatic Treasury percentage subvention. 'Block grants', reads the opening phrase of their pamphlet, 'lead directly to reduced expenditure. In all the discussions, going back forty years and more, nobody has queried the fact. Of the proposed block grant no less than $85–87\frac{1}{2}\%$ will be money hitherto paid out as percentage grant for education.' The whole history of 'permissive' legislation bears this out. Between the two wars it was permissible to any local education authority to raise the school-leaving age if they could raise the money required. Not one did so, until the age was raised by national legislation in 1946. Under the Fisher Act of 1918 local education authorities were permitted to establish compulsory part-time education for those who had left school; this could have been the beginning of county colleges, but only a few authorities tried it and only in Rugby did it survive. Yet these two areas of expansion are now confirmed by the Crowther Report as our prime requirements. The belief that local control means local authorities prepared to spend money more freely than the central government, and vying with each other to produce the best school system, is perhaps based on a misreading of American experience. It is true that America comes only second to Russia in the proportion of the national income devoted to education, and that in rich upper-middle-class districts local taxation supports a magnificent school system. Against that must be seen a picture of ill-paid and insecure teachers and wide areas of sub-standard education in the poorer states. And the gerrymandering of school-board boundaries to ensure that middle-class taxes support middle-class education distorts the picture still further.

FREEDOM THROUGH CENTRALIZATION

That a Liberal view of education should in the end favour an extension of the power of the central government may seem at first odd. But it would not be the first time that an extension of central power at the expense of local powers was the way to freedom. As soon as one is prepared to question the dogma that education in England and Wales is a function of the general purpose local government structure, a number of other possible advantages of a national system become apparent. One is in the whole recuitment, training, deployment, and status of teachers. We have at least, as some localized systems have not, a common standard of pay for teachers. But the fiction that this is reached by an agreement between the representatives of the local education authorities and the teachers' organizations in the Burnham Committee, with the Minister of Education as a benevolent observer, has been finally exposed by the recent decision on the salary pause. The Minister is the chief paymaster, through grants to the local authorities, and everyone knows by now that the most important factor in the 'negotiations' is the amount of money that the Minister is prepared to make available. Training of teachers, particularly if it is to be integrated more closely with higher education in general, might well become a national rather than a local responsibility. There are, besides, all sorts of comparatively small but not wholly unimportant points in connection with the terms of service of teachers, secondment for refresher courses for instance, or security for re-appointment for those who undertake service overseas, in which at present local authorities differ in their attitude. At present, for instance, the Minister, having drawn up an excellent code for secondment of teachers overseas, concludes with a paragraph beginning 'The Minister is confident that authorities will do their best to offer the assurances afforded by the code'.[1] It is perfectly open for the Finance Committee of Bottington Borough Council to decide that the ratepayers cannot afford it; or for the council as a whole to decide that Bottington is short of teachers anyway and that secondment overseas is a bad thing. Would it not be a great saving of man-hours and a much more satisfactory situation for the teaching profession if instead of 'negotiating' with 149 different education authorities, or expressing 'hope' and 'confidence', the Ministry of Education could lay down clear and generally applicable regulations? It might be going too far to adopt the Russian system for dealing with the problem of 'teacher-shortage' areas, and compel all newly qualified teachers to serve their first two years in the post to which they are allotted – though in many other government services and for many teachers in other countries this is a commonplace. But would we not be getting nearer to a solution if, instead of 149 authorities from Eastbourne to Walsall competing for the teachers' services (even with the quota system limiting this competition), all publicly appointed teachers, though appointed by the school governors or local authority, were members of one national education service? The rights of the teacher against undue control or exploitation by his national employer could surely be safeguarded as those of the doctor have been. No one would suggest making such radical changes in our educational system lightly, and in any case the procedures which would be necessary to introduce them if, on balance, they seemed desirable, need much more detailed study than they have yet received. This would appear exactly the sort of issue that calls for a Royal Commission. It is one where most of the fact finding will already have been done by the Crowther, Robbins and Newsome Committees, and where the administrative authorities concerned, whether national or local, are in some sense parties to the dispute. The appointment

---

[1] Ministry of Education Circular 10/60 (September 1960).

of a Commission with wide terms of reference and with a membership of widely varying experiences, to investigate the whole structure of the educational system, and on whose recommendations a new and radical Education Act could be planned, should, in my opinion, be the first step in a Liberal policy for education. Even with the preliminary work which has been done it would probably take at least two years, particularly if, as in the days of Matthew Arnold, the Commission were to send some senior inspectors to study the educational systems of our neighbours. Pressure for the appointment of such a Commission to review the whole structure and administration of English education should start now.

PART FIVE

A Policy for Science

IAN E. BUSH

'The man who proportions the several parts of a mill uses the same scientific principles as if he had power of constructing an universe' – Thomas Paine, *The Age of Reason* (1795).

'Comment oser parler des lois du hasard?' – Bertrand, *Calcul des Probabilités*.

The certainty and clarity of Thomas Paine's outlook on the world and its affairs was allied to a Platonic conception of science which would be rejected by most scientists and philosophers today. His ideas on the application of scientific knowledge, however, lose nothing by their Realist enthusiasm, and the passage quoted above is striking in that it could have been written by Francis Bacon or, just as well, spoken by Lord Hailsham as Minister for Science. The applications of scientific knowledge are now widely appreciated, and in fact it is these applications which most people refer to today when they talk of 'science'. The place of science in modern society, however, is not fully embraced by this sense of the term. Nevertheless, Paine's statement clearly represents our modern realization that science is an activity of sufficient importance to deserve not only the material support but, to some extent at least, the control and direction of governments.

The other aspects of science are very little understood or appreciated by the bulk of humanity. But, in the long run, they are probably more important than any of the more obvious technical and material ones that are so widely publicized. They are introduced, even if somewhat elliptically, by Bertrand's opening to his great work on the theory of probability. I shall be extremely hesitant in dealing with this side of science, but I shall plead that it should be the most important duty of anyone formulating policy to imitate my hesitancy and, above all, to pinch himself hard to see that he goes on doing so. Any policy for science, in fact, must somehow reconcile the two sides of the picture that are hinted at in these two quotations.

The skill and probity of most popular writers about science, including some of the greatest scientists themselves, has become so remarkable over the last thirty years that it may seem unreasonable to claim that the popular understanding of science, even in educated circles, is still extremely superficial. It will perhaps lessen the blow, however, if I point out that the nature of the scientific method and the manifold variety of scientific activities make up a complex which is not fully comprehended by very many scientists themselves. Lay understanding of science is superficial, and this statement applies as much to politicians and statesmen as to the majority of men and women who vote for or against them. The well-informed critic fulfils a valuable function. But ten years of reading the *Reader's Digest* is no substitute for a good medical degree, and a real understanding of Swiss law is best learnt from a Swiss lawyer, even if we might learn still more with a legal historian present to see fair play, or by going to several Swiss lawyers instead of one.

THE NATURE OF SCIENTIFIC METHOD

The most powerful argument against the idea that the true nature of science is easy to grasp is that most philosophers have given up trying to do so officially. The honesty of this self-discipline is perhaps our strongest reason for continuing to believe in their eventual salvation. A further argument is that, of those few who have had reasonable success, the majority were trained in science or mathematics to a degree that allowed them to understand and work with the theorems and methods of science as skilfully and as thoroughly as natural scientists themselves.

The philosophers, in fact, tend to get stuck precisely because they work with what is essentially the popular notion of the method of scientists. This notion is that the scientist starts with a set of observations of events ('facts'), derives therefrom a theory ('induction'), deduces further previously unobserved 'facts' from his theory, and then confirms his theory by finding that these 'facts' indeed exist, or drops it when he finds that these 'facts' do not apparently exist, in the real world. More recently, it has been realized that this is rather naïve, and it is customary to make the point that of course the scientist must have a theory to start with, or he could not have a frame of reference with which to make his observations of 'facts'. While this subtlety is quite correct, it gets no nearer the heart of the matter and is not much more than taking the side of the chicken rather than the egg.

The trouble from the philosopher's point of view is that the method contains within it the step of making a theory or hypothesis, and that the only way of classifying or defining this step has been to consider it as a case of induction. Now it is well known that more philosophers have taken to Scotch or been drummed out of the Athenaeum for trying to pass off an unsatisfactory theory of induction on their colleagues than could get through the eye of a needle in a month of Sundays; apparently it can't be done. The philosophers were, in fact, misled by the apparent success of the process in the hands of scientists; to be so successful it had to be logical in some way or another and the only logical process working in this direction had been called 'induction' even though it was recognized that the logic of induction had never been solved. Some philosophers even felt that the success of scientific 'induction' meant that some day their Prince *would* come.

The most succinct and utterly explicit solution of this apparent difficulty was provided by Karl Popper in *The Logic of Scientific Discovery,* first published in German in 1934. The elucidation of the main part of the problem is contained in the first ninety-two pages of the English edition of 1959. Popper arrives at his solution by a rigorous exclusion of any considerations other than those of what scientists actually do. As he says (p. 31), '... the work of the scientist consists in putting forward and testing theories', and he demonstrates quite clearly that previous philosophers have tied themselves up by trying to analyse scientific statements in terms of linguistic and logical categories bearing little or no relation to actual life. Proceeding on what are essentially sociological lines, he observes that the way in which scientists make theories is very various; it is useless to try and make out that this process conforms to any single type of logical step. It is clear that in many cases scientific theories are made with no more subtlety than is exhibited by a harassed lodger in an unfamiliar house trying to work out where the fuse-box is placed. In others, the steps can only be followed by a few dozen mathematicians in any one country.

Popper concludes that the unique success of the method of scientists must lie elsewhere, and that there is no single logical classification of the scientist's way of making theories. The secret lies, he believes, in the type of theory that scientists use and in the way in which such theories are used. The characteristic feature of scientific theories is that they are framed in such a way as to give the greatest possible opportunity of being disproved or, more accurately, falsified. The characteristic feature of the scientific method as a whole is the existence of a firmly based habit of frequent alternation between the activities of making theories and of testing them experimentally.

The real nature of this process is concealed by the phraseology of many scientific papers and by the emphasis of popular scientific writing on 'successful' results, either those *confirming* exciting and interesting theories or leading to technical and material advances. Thus the statement common in scientific papers, 'These results confirm X . . .' means 'These results are expected if the theory X is true, and we looked for these results in particular, because it was highly unlikely that we would obtain them if X were not true. Having obtained them, we have failed to falsify X.' What is not obvious to the non-scientist, even if he is aware of this translation, is the response that this sort of statement calls forth in other scientists. The real nature of the response lies in its balance; that is to say, the agreement of the scientific community as a whole to see that a theory calls forth an appropriate number of potentially falsifying experimental tests, and that a given set of experimental results calls forth a continuing effort to improve (in Popper's sense) old theories and produce new ones. Any one member of the scientific community may specialize in one or other of the two chief phases of the activity; some are brilliant at making theories, some at finding new deductions from old theories that make sharper tests, some at improving the experimental testing of existing theories, and so on. Most good scientists take a hand in all phases of the work.

It is important that this concept of the scientific method be widely understood, for it is probably the source of many misunderstandings. In the first place, it is hard for the layman to believe that scientific controversies are very different from other types of arguments, friendly or unfriendly, that take place in his daily life. It also shows us why the making of scientific theories often involves an imaginative process seeming like that of a poet or painter, but equally often seems more like the operation of a calculating machine. It goes a long way towards explaining why popular understanding of the scientific method is rarely more than superficial; the oscillations between deductive and theory-constructing activity that are made by a scientist in considering the simplest problem are so rapid and so numerous, and involve so many highly sophisticated and difficult turns of thought, that only a fully trained scientist can appreciate more than a very small fraction of them.

The nature of the scientific process is essential to any discussion of a policy for science. It will not have escaped the reader that the arguments above come very close to what is generally considered a highly dangerous and thoroughly illiberal outlook on human affairs, and one which is contrary to one of the most prominent principles of British politics. These arguments seem to suggest that in science the specialist is supreme and that science is a field in which the best 'general' education fails to provide an adequate basis for understanding and criticising it. In view of the critical importance of essentially scientific decisions to the everyday life of nations, it would seem to follow that this is a field of government in which national survival demands that we revoke the hallowed political principle that Ministerial chairs must be occupied by well-educated amateurs and not by axe-grinding specialists. Put baldly, the first idea is offensive to many popular apologists in the fields of letters, art, law, politics, and education. It is of the greatest political importance that the idea be accepted, for once the sense of offence has been dissipated, it will more easily be seen that the conclusions to be drawn from it are not as disastrous as might appear. The solution that is required is a radical one but quite simple; it contains within it the only possible answer to the pressing question: 'Who can be trusted to take the political decisions that are consequent upon scientific knowledge?"

THE PLACE OF SCIENCE IN NATIONAL LIFE

The problem of the Two Cultures put by C. P. Snow in a famous Rede Lecture is quite as serious as he suggests, and no mere talking point for cocktail parties. The political deductions to be drawn from his thesis have been clearly stated, but they have become confused by their connections with other controversies over higher education, with scientific policy in war, and by what seems to be a common misinterpretation of the deductions he himself made in his Harvard lectures on the Tizard-Cherwell controversy.[1] I shall concentrate on trying to remove the principal obstacle to accepting what is most important in them.

The essence of these two striking lectures can be summed up as follows.

1. An inability to understand the basic methods and conclusions of science is as uncultured today as it would have been thirty

[1] *Science and Government* (1961).

years ago not to have read Shakespeare, Browning, Proust, Gibbon, Adam Smith, or Keats.

2. The political consequences of the incorrect application of scientific knowledge to a large number of spheres of national life are so serious nowadays that the government and its departments, councils, and committees must be liberally staffed with men trained in science. Scientific advice to governments on a personal or caucus basis is no longer reliable, and indeed has already come very near proving disastrous in our recent history.

3. To avoid the risks of a serious waste of national resources or of mistakes fatal to our actual survival, we must see that our recruitment of politicians and administrators is altered so as to provide these men. Our pattern of education must be changed so as to make this possible.

I believe that Snow is right in the main, and that the only solution to this pressing problem is to be found in a re-phrasing of his first point. We must somehow ensure that a 'general' education includes scientific thought as completely and naturally as our present general basis of education includes a training in the three 'R's' and a knowledge of English literature, European and world history, geography, a foreign language, Christian scriptures, and sport. At university level, it must become the natural habit to think of a science degree as being just as obvious a pathway to politics, business, or administration as an arts degree. At postgraduate level, a three-year period doing research for a Ph.D. or M.Sc. must become as natural a preliminary for the civil service, politics, or a sales department in commerce, as a period of apprenticeship in business, accountancy, law, or journalism. At the outset it should be emphasized that this is not necessarily to be taken as a plea for 'general science' courses or degrees; this would miss the point completely, and in fact contradicts the whole thesis – which is that what we want is a real understanding of science, and not one that is watered down. There is little justification for supposing that a science degree actually lessens a man's capacity for playing a part in ordinary life.

There are many obstacles to our accepting this suggestion. But the main one is probably a partly justifiable suspicion that Snow is claiming that 'Anything you can do, scientists can do better'. This is a highly inflammatory suggestion. It was probably this, more than anything else, which led to such an extraordinary outburst in A. J. P. Taylor's review of Snow's book,[1] and his otherwise inexplicable failure as a trained historian to see what Snow was demanding. In fact, Snow's claim does not depend upon such a suggestion, even if he does sometimes sound as if he were guilty of making it. The point is that we are accustomed by years of tradition, not utterly devoid of the customary flavouring of one-upmanship, to think that science positively cripples a man for life as far as general affairs are concerned. It is this attitude that leads to remarks such as, 'Scientists must be on tap but not on top', or to the pathetic lapse of an ex-Prime Minister when he referred to some of the world's most brilliant physicists by an analogy of 'garage mechanics' in an article in the *Observer* a year ago. When looked at objectively, it is strange that an activity which is recognized to have been the main training and inspiration of some of the world's greatest geniuses should be thought to be a positive disadvantage in the application of intelligence to general affairs.

The plea that has become obscured in this controversy is not that scientists must be associated even more closely with government than hitherto, but that, since a close association is accepted as essential in many spheres, this association must involve a larger number of scientifically trained men than in the past. In other words, we can no longer afford to risk the idiosyncrasies of scientific opinion in governmental circles, any more than we risk the personal idiosyncrasies of lawyers, businessmen, soldiers, and civil servants there. It is the system of the recent past which in fact threatens to place axe-grinding specialists in the real seats of power. A Liberal policy should ensure that the influence of scientists is made democratic, so that it flows through as many channels as it does in other professional bodies.

Snow's 'deepest reason' for wanting more scientists in all levels of government is one, however, which does imply a superiority of scientists. Snow holds that Western society lacks foresight, in the sense that we are not as forward-looking or flexible in outlook as we ought to be. 'We seem to be flexible, but we haven't any model of the future before us,' he says (*Science and Government*, p. 80). He thinks that scientists, including both engineers and scientists 'proper', 'include a number of speculative and socially

[1] *Observer*, 9 April 1961.

imaginative minds' (ibid., p. 80) and that they 'have it within them to know what a future-directed society feels like, for science itself, in its human aspect, is just that'. This is undoubtedly a claim of a certain kind of superiority, and it is unavoidably one which will annoy all non-scientists. In fairness to Snow, however, it must be pointed out that he is careful to state: 'I am not saying, of course, that all scientists have foresight and no one else has. Foresight is a fairly rare quality' (ibid., p. 81).

There is no absolute standard of foresight, and we must examine Snow's contention by comparing the evidence of foresight among scientists, who by tradition are not admitted to spheres of general political influence, and to spheres of specialist influence only in small numbers, with the evidence of foresight among those professional classes who are. This is difficult to do thoroughly and objectively. But there can be very little doubt that there is no solid evidence *contradicting* Snow's contention, and plenty of evidence that scientists are no worse than others. This alone would be sufficient to make us question the present situation in which scientists are almost totally absent from political and general administrative circles. The world we see around us has been produced largely by the political thoughts and actions of 'men of affairs', either self-taught or with arts degrees; it can scarcely be considered an outstanding tribute to the foresight or quality of thought and feeling possessed by such men. Even if the intimate knowledge of the frontiers of science were not so necessary in the contemplation of the future of our world as it is today, one might wonder whether it would not be wise to look around for further advice. Such distortions as: 'Scientists of the younger generation hold that anyone who shows foresight should be locked up',[1] are alone sufficient to make us extremely chary of accepting the wisdom and foresight of the non-scientist on trust.

Let us take just one example of Taylor's misleading picture from this article: 'The story of nuclear physics is throughout a poor tribute to the foresight of scientists. They guessed at random according to their personal or political inclination, from Teller's obsessive anti-Bolshevism at one end of the scale to Max Born's near pacifism at the other.' The first sentence betrays either an extraordinary ignorance or else a distortion hard to understand in a professional historian. The discovery of nuclear fission was

[1] A. J. P. Taylor, *Observer*, op. cit.

made in small-scale experiments just before the second World War and rapidly confirmed. On the basis of two scientific papers extant in the journals of 1939–40, every nuclear physicist of the top rank in every country having such scientists saw at once that Rutherford's prediction that nuclear energy would be impossible to unleash was invalidated, and that this energy might be produced in the form of destructive weapons in the foreseeable future. No one other than these physicists saw this possibility. Szilard, Einstein, and their colleagues in the United States went one step further; they recognized that the magnitude of such weapons would undoubtedly prove decisive to any country which first succeeded in producing them. Impelled by their horror, and personal experience, of Nazism they managed to impress upon President Roosevelt the desperate nature of their conclusion. It is interesting to look back at this stage and realize that it took a long letter from Einstein himself and personal pressure via Leonard Sachs to secure even an interview with Roosevelt. Even this farsighted statesman betrayed by his relatively casual attitude towards agreeing to this crucial interview that he was unconscious of the potential importance of the political and economic effects of scientific advances.

Thus, within months of the crucial scientific papers, naturally hesitant to thrust themselves into the unfamiliar world of political pressure in which they were totally inexperienced, these physicists had the foresight and courage not only to press their view but to realize that the subject had to be put before the President of the United States himself and to overcome great obstacles in order to do so.

Later, when the atomic bomb had been built, the question arose of how it should be used. The American military authorities and a limited number of the principal scientists in the project wanted to use it on a Japanese city. The majority of scientists in the project viewed this policy with horror and, on being asked for their views, pointed out in the Franck report the consequences of such a use of the bomb. It was this step which produced Lord Attlee's notorious comment that this was like asking one's garage mechanic for advice on the best road to York. Every prediction of the political and economic consequences of this action made by Franck and his colleagues came true. Following the rejection of the Franck report by President Truman and his military colleagues, the nuclear physicists took a further step. They founded the *Bulletin of the Atomic Scientists*, and in the following ten years played a very large part in the education of the public on the nature and consequences of nuclear weapons.

It can scarcely be said that justice has been done to this story by Taylor's first sentence above, or by his subsequent statement: 'As nuclear weapons developed, scientists have shown much casualness and irresponsibility but, with a few honourable exceptions (including Sir Charles Snow), little foresight.' Taylor's objection simply tells us that scientists, like other human beings, exhibit a wide spectrum of temperaments and political beliefs, and that in putting scientific knowledge to practical use, there is a large area of possibilities which can be argued about. This confirms the idea that democratic safety is only to be found in numbers, and that where decisions have such critical consequences, safety is even more important than in other fields of action.

There are many other areas in which the foresight of scientists has been strikingly evident: strikingly, because so often it has not been their professional duty to lead the field. It was almost entirely due to Blackett and his scientific colleagues that, by the end of the second World War, the whole approach to tactics and strategy had been revolutionized by the development of Operational Research.[1] It took several years of struggle, however, before the Services accepted willingly the conclusions of these scientists, which were responsible for an enormous increase in military efficiency, not the least being our ability to win by a small margin the war against the U-boat. It should be emphasized that this was not a matter simply of weapons and gadgets, it was largely a question of how men and existing weapons were most efficiently deployed and of deciding which new types of weapon or gadget were likely to prove most valuable. This was a field, then, in which scientists were not only better than non-scientists as a whole, but better than their Service 'employers' who were specially trained in that field.

Scientists also have a passable record in other matters. At a time when A. L. Rowse was infuriated and disgusted by the complacency of the 'men of affairs' who visited All Souls at week-ends, Lindemann himself was making trips to Germany and arranging

[1] Cf. e.g. *Science at War*, HMSO (1947).

the escapes of scientists in danger of persecution; and Tizard was ensuring that we were possessed of the apparatus without which we could not have won the Battle of Britain. While the majority of English opinion was blind to the meaning of Nazism, scientists in England and America were playing a more active part than most in finding positions for refugee German scientists, and at the beginning of the second World War they, more than any other group, went to war with a will. It was the initiative of scientists that led to the setting up of the Department of Scientific and Industrial Research and of the Medical and Agricultural Research Councils; that led and maintained the post-war movement for academic freedom (cf. *Science and Freedom*); that has played a large part in impressing upon the public the urgent need to encourage technological progress throughout the world.[1]

Scientists have no monopoly of foresight or wisdom, as Snow has already pointed out. On the other hand, in the face of the recent, and even current, underestimation of the potentialities of scientists in our national and international life, one must insist firmly that they are at least as well qualified in general affairs as non-scientists, and Snow may perhaps be forgiven if he occasionally seems to claim more than this. Most scientists are well aware that for every Einstein, Tizard, Blackett, Dale, Adrian, or Polanyi, there is a Roosevelt, Churchill, Beveridge, Cripps, Bevin, or Lansbury. Non-scientists sometimes write as if Fuchs, Pontecorvo, and Nunn-May existed while Burgess, Maclean, and Blake did not. It is also sometimes forgotten that you cannot exclude a large professional group from the general political life of a country for half a century in which the activities of that group have transformed the world, and then complain that they 'make a mess of things' while 'we poor chaps – whom you condemn as scientifically illiterate – have to clear it up' (A. J. P. Taylor, ibid.). We owe it to the wisdom of an anonymous non-scientist that most of us do *not* expect to have our cake and eat it.

A Liberal policy for science must first take account of the general question of the place of science in our national life. This is the major background against which all more detailed questions of how scientific research is to be supported and how the balance between applied and fundamental research is to be struck, have to be considered. The pre-eminence of scientists in the academic

[1] *The Advancement of Science*, Vol. 54 (1947).

world; of science as a factor shaping all aspects of our world; the very number of intelligent and imaginative men and women taking part in scientific work; the critical importance of scientific discovery for our economic and political survival – these must be accepted as the indisputable facts they are. Having accepted them, we must recognize that the present political position of science is not only failing to make it an integral part of our democratic processes, but that this failure is dangerous for our political health. The bogey of the specialist in the Minister's chair is simply due to the fact that as a nation, and in common with many others, we fail to realize that science is part of general culture and not just a matter of specialist technique.

Some recognition of the problem already exists, and it is to be hoped that the moves already set on foot will grow and have a desirable influence on our affairs. A Minister for Science has been appointed and the honours bestowed upon scientists are increasingly obvious and noticed. On the other hand, one of our major political parties showed its lack of consciousness of the issue by suggesting the appointment of a Minister for Science rather late in the last General Election campaign, and concentrated on a rather limited appeal to the sectional interests of scientists. On all sides the clamour for trained men, largely in fields of science or mathematics, rises to a desperate crescendo, but there is little sign that the Government is anxious to meet the educational problem in the way that is needed, or even going to do so under pressure. Even on the more limited issue of scientific and technical manpower, that is to say the issue of scientists and engineers working at their customary lasts, it is a striking sign of the times that the recent report of Political and Economic Planning was entirely innocent of any serious mention of this topic.[1]

A Liberal policy should attempt to solve these problems as rapidly and urgently as possible while paying close attention to the existing framework of governmental scientific bodies. While setting out to influence the educational policy of the country, to encourage the employment of scientifically trained men in business, administration, the armed services, and politics, the Government Research Councils should be kept as autonomous as possible and the Advisory Council on Scientific Policy should continue in its present role. If this were done, the experience and advice of

[1] Cf. *Nature*, 15 April 1961.

the existing bodies should be of considerable value during the planning and carrying out of these policies.

The main steps to be taken in this part of a Liberal policy for science should include the following. First, the Minister for Science should be made a full member of the Cabinet and should be a scientist of considerable experience and quality, preferably with a mixture of academic experience and of work in industry or in a government establishment. His senior permanent staff should include at least two other first-class scientists and one first-class man with legal or financial training. Although better than nothing, a non-scientist Minister backed up by scientists retains too much of the old situation of 'scientists on tap'. With full Cabinet status, a scientific Minister would be possessed of all the information and all the restraints on specialist idosyncrasy that accrue to such a position; there would also be little opportunity and no excuse for intrigue. The Minister would also be able to influence those spheres in which he should indeed exert an influence, namely education, trade and industry, the armed services, economic policy, cultural exchange, and scientific and technical research.

The next steps should be in the field of education. The most urgent problem is to provide teachers of mathematics and science for primary and secondary schools. This will be difficult to do without breaking some eggs. It is simply one of many aspects of the general problem that the balance is at present unhealthily in favour of industry in the competition for all types of skilled personnel. Any attempt to make industry's competitive position less favourable will be criticized as hindering the expansion and improvement of the economy; on the other hand, selective increases in the salary scales of teachers of science and mathematics will be greatly resented by the great majority of teachers. The gravity of the present situation can hardly be over-emphasized however; on the national scale we have been guilty over the last ten years of the cardinal mistake of failing to plough back enough into investment for the future.

An important part of the educational efforts of a Minister for Science, however, should be to bring science into the curricula for students who are not going to be teachers of science or research workers. The existing efforts of radio and television broadcasting, of the general press, and of the *New Scientist* in particular should receive every encouragement. An important question to be gone

10

into is whether 'general science' courses should be encouraged and whether specialization in science in sixth forms should be reduced. This is a highly controversial field; unfortunately, appeals for less specialization and for general science courses have come largely from non-scientists and have often irritated the scientists. It is widely thought, however, that many features of the present system are unsatisfactory. Thus, for instance, most sixth form courses in science carry a student well into the first-year syllabus of most university degrees and sometimes beyond it; this is true also for some non-scientific subjects. It is quite clear that either this should be avoided or else that Honours courses at least should start at a much higher standard. An even greater problem is that of higher education for industrial tasks; the apprentice system is hopelessly inadequate for the needs of today.[1]

Many other opportunities exist for a Minister for Science to exert a useful influence. He could see that Royal Commissions and government enquiries are provided with scientific members; that nationalized industries and firms in which the government is an important shareholder appoint a reasonable number of scientifically trained men to their Boards; that the offices of the government departments employ scientists, particularly those experienced in operational research. Not the least important part of his efforts might be directed to seeing that the Duke of Edinburgh, who has made several extremely far-sighted and imaginative contributions to the problems under discussion, should be encouraged to give his support in stimulating the public to consider these matters rather than discouraged as soon as he becomes in the slightest degree controversial.

SCIENCE IN RESEARCH AND DEVELOPMENT

The general position of science in our national life should be our major concern because, to re-phrase the epigram, we shall not get enough scientists of the best quality 'on tap' unless *some* scientists are 'on top'. With one or two exceptions, it has been recognized in recent years that this country is endangered by its present lack of trained scientists in research and development, and by the shortage of teachers of mathematics and science in the schools. In addition, many industries have been dangerously slow to undertake research and to employ well-qualified scientists and engineers

[1] See e.g. Andrew Shonfield, *Observer*, 4 June 1961.

on research and development. A Liberal policy for science would undoubtedly have to take immediate action on this question.

In discussing a policy for science in its conventional sphere of operation, we cannot do much better than consider the first report of the Advisory Council on Scientific Policy which was made on matters specifically recommended for their consideration by Lord Hailsham as the first Minister for Science; that is, their report for 1959–60 (HMSO). The Council reported that British gross expenditure on research and development is the same fraction of the gross national product as that in the United States. Although this represents an increase of 40% in the period between 1955 and 1959, it is hardly encouraging. First of all, there is no law which gives us at present a sure guide to what this fraction ought to be; no one would be happy if they were told that the fractional cost of the plumbing and heating of hospitals was the same as that of railway stations. Second, there are a number of arguments that suggest that the figure should be higher for small highly industrialized countries than for those with a large fraction of their gross product in the form of raw materials and agricultural produce. This figure, then, is one which by itself is not altogether reassuring.

The detailed examination by the report of current British activity in research and development is far from reassuring and in many places extremely critical. When the views of other scientists, particularly the younger ones, and the views of independent bodies are taken into account, the picture is gloomy. The Council points out a number of fields of fundamental research in which too little is being done in this country; apart from their intrinsic value, some of these fields, for example seismology, oceanography, and pure mathematics, have applications which may rapidly expand at any moment and place an impossible strain on our present resources. In the field of applied science and technology, the Council is surprisingly critical for a committee of this type; it believes that there is 'a serious deficiency over the whole field' of civil engineering, and numerous inadequacies in the field of veterinary research. After this pessimistic review, it is slightly surprising that the Council leans over backwards in suggesting that in the technological field the required impetus must come from industry and is not the responsibility of the government. This is strange (at any rate from a politically independent Council) because the report notes with disappointment that the offer of the Department of Scientific and Industrial Research in 1958 to consider proposals from industry for support of research by development contracts has been almost totally disregarded by industry so far.

It must be remembered that this report is from a Council justifiably prone to weigh its words rather carefully. Furthermore, a number of its members (nine out of the fifteen) occupy positions on the Research Councils or other official bodies which will prevent them from giving their opinions as freely or strongly as they might otherwise do. When we examine the opinions or findings of the more independent persons or bodies which have gone into these matters, the views become more critical and are expressed much more strongly. It is sometimes claimed that such views tend to be partial and to give an incomplete picture of the situation, but it must be remembered that the information upon which such opinions are based is not easy to collect and to a large extent we are forced to rely on partial expressions of opinion, since there are no bodies in existence with the staff and facilities to make a comprehensive investigation. Such an enquiry would be a major piece of research.

The report, published in March 1960, by the Institute of Physics and the Physical Society on the subject of the postgraduate training of physicists in British universities is particularly disturbing. The distinguished committee which produced it concluded that even in this doyen of the sciences there was a serious inadequacy in the postgraduate training facilities for physicists in this country, and that there is no hope of remedying the situation unless the University Grants Committee and the DSIR are prepared to make large increases in their financial support to universities so as to enable the increase of the staffs of university departments and the provision of an extra year's study for students in these departments. In view of an ever-present tendency to emphasize and admit our deficiencies in applied science while complacently maintaining that 'of course' Britain continues to reign supreme in fundamental work and in originality of ideas, it is unpleasant to read that lack of originality, and of flexibility and adaptability, were consistently criticized by industrial and other employers of young physicists in this country.

In the field of mathematics and in certain fields of applied science, independent comment has recently taken on a dangerously desperate note. Professor Coulson has recently drawn attention to the almost desperate situation in the teaching of mathematics[1] and even the sober report of the Civil Service Commissioners (1959–60, HMSO) expressed concern over the inadequate numbers of suitable chemists, physicists, engineers, and mathematicians applying for entry to the Civil Service, claiming that 'the situation has worsened and the present position now gives rise to grave disquiet'. This body covers a sufficiently wide field that they also complain of the lack of good candidates with training in law and psychology and, as suggested earlier in this essay, attribute the whole picture to the 'serious shortage of good recruits to the professional and technical classes'. In connection with seismology, the Advisory Council on Scientific Policy itself adopts strong language: 'Superficially, the United Kingdom appears to have an adequate number of seismological stations . . .; but most of them contain only old instruments which are incapable of making the type of records now required for many recent developments.' Earlier it states: 'Our present position calls for urgent consideration, the more so as our weakness has been underlined by our need to seek advice outside the United Kingdom on problems arising at the recent Geneva Conference and by the requirements of the proposed development of international inspection and control schemes for nuclear explosions.'

Two counter-arguments have been put forward by critics, although they are a very small minority of those who have pronounced on this situation. The first was most strikingly put by Professor Jewkes (British Association Meeting, 1959), who claimed that since the salary scales for scientists had risen at the same rate (or even rather more slowly in certain cases) as the average for the last ten years, it was unreasonable to claim that the need for scientists was not being met.[2]

Professor Blackett has already pointed out both the doubtful nature of this conclusion and the frailty of the argument which led to it; the wide application of this argument would lead to the conclusion that the need for teachers, doctors, midwives, and librarians had been steadily and rapidly declining over the last ten years, and it appears to rest on outdated economic

[1] *New Scientist*, 1 June 1961.
[2] *New Scientist*, 17 December 1959, and subsequent correspondence.

theory as well as upon ignorance of science and scientists. It is a reflection of our national disregard for the future that government policy (by both major parties) has consistently neglected the *increasing* need for highly trained professional men in all spheres in a small manufacturing country in the twentieth century, and in doing so has failed to remember that these professional groups have either no trade organizations or ones which have only recently learned from the experience of the last fifteen years that politeness never impressed a politician. It is only in very recent years that a majority of these professional classes have even overcome their traditional aversion to discussing questions of salary in public.

The other argument is that our present deficiencies are due to the failure of universities in particular, and of the professions themselves in general, to adapt their ideas and practices to modern conditions. Universities have come under special criticism for failing to expand sufficiently rapidly and for inefficiency, both in their administration and in their teaching. These critics suppose either that a policy for science must wait upon individual initiative, or that it should simply force the universities and professions into more efficient moulds. In certain respects, these criticisms are partly justified. But over the field as a whole they cannot be accepted, and in some ways they represent a gross insult to the universities and to professional scientists. In actual fact, scientists and academics were among the first to point out the growing seriousness of the situation; the first to welcome proposals to expand the university student population; and some of the most active in continuing to warn the public and the politicians of the true situation. Nor have the older men been the only contributors; the recent policy statement of the Association of Scientific Workers, whose members are largely young non-professorial scientists both in and outside universities, is an admirable example of the hard work being done spontaneously by scientists to draw public attention to the grave deficiencies of our present educational capacity in the fields of mathematics and science.[1]

On the simple question of manpower, the Committee on Scientific Manpower of the Advisory Council on Scientific Policy reported in 1956 and again in 1959 (Cmd 902) and its findings are unequivocally in support of the contention that we are not pro-

[1] *Science and Education*, A.Sc.W. (1960).

ducing nearly enough scientists, engineers, and mathematicians. In the first place, they report that if employers had been able to fill their vacancies at the beginning of 1959, the total number of scientists employed would have exceeded the Committee's 1956 estimate of the requirement for 1959. The grand total of qualified scientists and engineers in January 1959 in Great Britain was 173,000. The Committee estimated that the total requirement in 1962 will have risen to 211,700, of whom 87,100 will be scientists and 124,600 engineers, and that to meet this need and cover wastage by retirement and emigration, 57,250 would have to be trained in the period 1959–62. In actual fact, about 51,650 were expected to qualify in this period on the basis of the expected expansion of technical colleges and universities. Thus we could expect to be short of these men and women to the tune of 5,600 by 1962 or about $2\frac{1}{2}\%$ of the required number. This appears to be a marginal deficit, but $2\frac{1}{2}\%$ of the desirable 212-thousand-odd represents three years' output of scientists and engineers from one whole medium-sized university, and over the three-year period under consideration it represents a deficit of 9% of the output desired over this period.

It is probable, however, that the deficit will be larger than this. Not only has every previous forecast of the need for scientific and technical personnel been an underestimate but, because of government parsimony, the rate of expansion of the universities has been slower over the last five years than was planned. In 1957, the clamour for an increase in expenditure on higher education and scientific research reached one of its recent climaxes. The only obvious result was that the University Grant for the 1957–62 Quinquennium was drastically cut and the chairman of the University Grants Committee actually advised some universities to cut back on research in terms that suggested that research was some form of dispensable perversion indulged in by university workers. There is little doubt that the consequences of under-estimating our needs in this field may prove disastrous to the economic health of this country for the next twenty years; as the report of the Association of Scientific Workers points out (ibid., p. 7), the only serious consequence of *overestimating* our needs would be 'a minor one: for the first time in a generation a number of scientists would enter the teaching profession'.

Unfortunately, there are many fields of science in which British scientists are their own worst enemies when attempting to arouse public and official opinion on this issue. Despite overwork due to impossible teaching duties, and lack of generous financial support, they still manage to turn out some of the best fundamental, and in certain fields applied, work in the world. This is particularly true in the biological and medical sciences. These are generally recognized to have been the branches of science most neglected by official policy; and here one must take issue with the Advisory Council on Scientific Policy, who have consistently stated that there was no serious shortage of workers in these fields. As a physiologist, I have left them to the end to avoid the semblance of special pleading, and because the grave situation in those branches which have at least had official support in the last ten years, the physical and engineering sciences, is far more disturbing. Although outstanding work is still being done in these fields in Great Britain, any young worker in them will confirm the view that the position is extremely weak as far as staff and breadth of work is concerned. Several large and wealthy drug firms have been forced to meet the crippling shortage of pharmacologists by sending chemists away for a year to receive training in this branch of biological science. I know of one medium-sized firm in which there is no trained pharmacologist in the entire biological control and toxicity departments. A recent survey[1] of the position of biochemistry in the country provided a good picture both of the poverty of university departments and the domination of this field by research institutes and outside support. Particularly valuable is the article by Professor Happold (ibid., p. 29) which is based on replies to a questionnaire from all but two of the Professors of Biochemistry in Redbrick Universities. One of his replies reads: '. . . if the apparatus which has been bought with gifts from the Royal Society, the Rockefeller Foundation, or the Medical Research Council were taken away from this department, I can safely say that every single major line of research at present being pursued here would stop at once. The department would not contain a single refrigerated centrifuge, we should have one quartz spectrophotometer, some balances and a good supply of chemicals and glassware.' It is even more serious when one considers the way in which some of the half dozen really outstanding pieces of biological

---

[1] *The Organization and Financing of Research in Biochemistry and Allied Sciences in Great Britain*, Biochemical Society (1960).

and medical research in the last ten years, of which we are rightly proud, have been financed. It is probable that but for the Rockefeller Foundation, the Nuffield Foundation, and the Medical Research Council, there would be little to boast about.

It is in physics and the biological sciences that emigration has been the most serious problem. There can be little doubt that the real figures are gloomier than official silences would have us believe, and that there have been attempts to conceal their true gravity. Thus after many official statements that the magnitude of the problem was not serious in 1958–9, it was somewhat ironical to discover in 1959 that the Atomic Energy Authority had started a campaign to try and attract back some of the scientists it had lost by emigration to the USA and Canada. It was disquieting to learn recently[1] that the campaign has been going on for two years but has had a very meagre result. The complacency of some official opinion on this issue is depressing; a favourite line is that only the mediocrities go, in the hope of finding it easier to get support for their work in the uncritical luxury of the American scene. Among these supposed mediocrities I know of four Fellows of the Royal Society who emigrated in the last three years (three to the USA); it is a commonplace that a very large number of young leading biochemists in Great Britain today owe a large measure of their present financial support in research (if it is from British sources) to emergency action taken by the authorities in the face of the otherwise certain threat of their emigration. In medicine the picture is complicated by special factors, but most opinion inclines to believe that official figures are underestimates.[2] Davison shows that it is practically certain that over the last five years an average of 220 doctors a year have emigrated to Canada alone – 'equivalent to the whole output of two medical schools'. In 1960, it is reported that there were more new registrations of emigrant British doctors in Victoria, Australia, than of Australians.

There can be little doubt that the situation is grave. When official opinion in published reports betrays definite anxiety or criticism, and independent opinion expressed in a large number of articles verges often on the frenetic, we can safely assume that the true position is certainly very serious and quite possibly threatens disaster if strong action is not taken at once. It is

[1] *Guardian*, 27 May 1961.
[2] See e.g. R. H. Davison, *Lancet*, 20 May 1961, p. 1107.

particularly disquieting that the DSIR report (1959–60, HMSO) confirms the views of many in other fields that nuclear physicists who emigrated to North America did so not simply for higher salaries but in the expectation of more generous support for their work and the stimulation of vigorous working conditions. They were apparently right in these expectations. A typical aspect of official shortsightedness is that there has been little public recognition of the fact that competition for scientists is international in character in a way that is true of no other field. The USA is far from complacent over the need for trained personnel and the expansion of research institutes and universities that has already been started is enormous. There appears to have been no official recognition of this fact.

The government's response to this situation is less than adequate. The problem is not only as serious as any other single problem of domestic policy: it affects the consideration of practically every feature of our economic and political future. One is hardly encouraged to hope for anything better to come when, shortly before the first strike of teachers in our history, the government produces a budget with heavy emphasis on reducing public expenditure and within months declares a subsidy of £30 million to support an industry whose export performance and failure to carry out research and development are notorious. The manpower problem now demands a number of 'crash' measures which will make the carrying out of a co-ordinated policy for science even more difficult than it would be at any time. Thanks to the lack of foresight of our two major political parties, the British public is again approaching a Dunkirk with that glorious complacency that can only be born of nearly complete ignorance.

FREEDOM AND DIRECTION IN SCIENCE

There is a considerable danger that British science, and with it British economic and political strength, will either decline because of a vicious circle of lack of support through economic weakness, leading to further economic weakness and further lack of support, and so on, or else that many of its better features will be sacrificed in the event of drastic measures being taken to save the situation. Even in 1958, the discussion of scientific emigration led to the publication of a small number of extremely reactionary opinions, including a few which raised openly the suggestion that such emigration might require restrictive controls. Although these suggestions represent the lunatic fringe, it is some indication of the political difficulties attending science that such a fringe should exist; public opinion at present possesses a very ambivalent image of the scientist which veers between stereotypes from the dull plodding laboratory man with no interests outside his work, colourless but 'safe'; to the Faustian genius who is not only unsafe but wicked. Because of public ignorance of science, these stereotypes are potentially dangerous; we cannot even rely upon so-called educated people to be immune from their influence during periods of sharp controversy or emergency. It is all the more important that those framing a Liberal policy for science should be aware of these dangers and forearmed with a firmly based understanding of the issues that are involved.

The first and most important problem facing us here is a confusion between the two concepts of science suggested by my opening quotations. Public and official opinion is now aware of the first concept but has great difficulty in accepting the second. The consequence is that everyone in science and technology is thought of as a 'scientist', and that it is very difficult for the ordinary man to understand that both the paths followed by pure science and the applications that arise from its findings are almost totally unpredictable, at any rate in detail. The discussion of this problem is further confused by the division between so-called pure and applied science. As in so many other instances, genuine differences exist between different branches of science and between applied and pure science as a whole, but these are simply the consequence of scientists being human beings and of the fluctuations of interest and quality in the different branches of a constantly developing set of human activities.

The problem has arisen essentially because pure science is now as expensive as applied science. The natural response of the politician is to demand that the money voted to support it be controlled in the same way as other public expenditure, but unfortunately this field is one in which it is impossible to see any measurable return for the money spent directly upon it, and quite impossible to predict the secondary consequences which might accrue, including financial risks of uncertain cost and outcome. Before this is fully understood, we must expect further attempts to 'increase the efficiency of', 'avoid wasteful expenditure on', 'avoid duplication in', 'encourage the most important fields of', research in pure and applied science, and we shall have to resist most or all of them. Pure and applied science are perhaps best considered as a continuous spectrum of activities without a sharp dividing line; furthermore activities in one part of the spectrum may have a profound and usually quite unpredictable effect upon activities not only in closely related fields *but upon all parts of the spectrum, however distant.* These effects can occur as the result of the interaction of purely scientific factors or as the result of political and economic consequences, or as a combination of all three. Let us take one chain of events as an example.

Fleming's activities in pure science made him interested in antibiotic substances of natural origin; his experience in the applied science of routine bacteriology sharpened an already considerable observational acuity so that he at once spotted the significance of a routine culture plate which had been spoiled by the chance alighting of a mould upon it. The potential applications were such as to stimulate him to culture the mould and demonstrate the presence of penicillin. Partly because of the lack of suitable techniques in another pure science, he was unable to isolate pure penicillin in quantities sufficient to make it a feasible therapeutic agent. The stimulus of wartime surgery and the further advance of biochemical techniques allowed Florey and Chain to produce it successfully. Partly because the Americans had perfected a technique in another applied science (deep culture of micro-organisms) the production of penicillin was undertaken by American drug firms. Largely as a result of this head-start, nearly all the subsequent major antibiotics were discovered and produced by American firms. It is undoubted that the profits from these activities were the main reason why many of these American firms were able to establish international organizations with several large branches in this country.

The cost of the American dominance in the field of antibiotics to our Health Service has been enormous. And this is not the end of the story. In 1950, one American company was about to bring to a stop a long and then unsuccessful search for micro-organisms that might produce useful chemical modifications of steroid hormones or their precursors. Quite by chance, a culture plate left lying on a window sill produced a growth of a fungal micro-organism, not previously known to the investigators, which was capable of adding a crucial hydroxyl group to a readily available steroid raw material, thus converting it at one step into a substance from which cortisone could easily and cheaply be synthesized. Because they had been drawn into the wartime manufacture of penicillin, this firm was able to put this process into almost immediate operation using the large fermenting towers that had previously been used for penicillin manufacture but which now lay idle. Because of this, an English drug firm starting with another raw material was forced to develop a completely different chemical method of synthesizing cortisone, a magnificent piece of work but one which was both costly and protracted.

The consideration of such chains of events and personal experience of them has led most scientists to the conclusion that prediction and control of scientific research, including even a fairly large slice of applied scientific work, is extremely hazardous to say the least. It is sometimes said that this type of progress appears to be so dependent upon chance that it suggests either that scientists are merely inspired followers of hunches, or that they have been too careless to plan their work in any other way. The first conclusion is used in current one-upmanship, the second is used to suggest that planned research has simply not been tried on a sufficient scale to show whether or not it would work, and that perhaps scientists themselves are not the best people to do the planning.

A Liberal policy should be based on the recognition that it is almost impossible to assess the financial value of pure research, and that any piece of applied research, however trivial its apparent beginnings, may have consequences of value over and above those originally hoped for, and quite independently of whether the explicit aims are achieved or not. In other words, the financial reward of any piece of research can only be assessed as a minimum figure; in successful applied research the eventual value is more likely to be slightly greater than this minimum than to be very much greater, while in pure research the eventual value, if it is calculable at all, is more likely to be very much greater than the original minimum assessment. Assuming that a reasonable fraction of research projects in applied science and technology will succeed in achieving their explicit aims, practical policy should take account of the fact that unexpected developments should arise at a rate proportional to the total amount of work going on. The combined value of these developments, however, depends not only upon their isolated use, but upon their combination with each other and with earlier or later work. It is clear then that the value accruing over the years from a given body of applied scientific research will be proportional not directly to the amount of work being done but to some power thereof. Any planning of applied scientific work should therefore be based on two main theorems:

(a) Relatively small increases or decreases in the amount of work achieved will over any moderate term of years be likely to cause large increases or decreases in the financial return from such work.

(b) The organization and planning of scientific research, once its scale has been determined, should be confined largely to seeing that, other things being equal, the maximum possibility of combining the results and experience of the individual projects is achieved, for upon this depends the value of the power term in the above simplified equation: i.e. the extent to which the return is greater than a simple proportion of the total work done.

The practical consequences of the first theorem are simply that no upper limit of expenditure on research should be fixed without good reasons, and that a minimum figure is more likely to be too low than too high. If we are going to try and 'speak of the laws of chance', then the rule must be to maximize our chances. The second theorem has a number of practical consequences, many of which could profitably be subjected to further research. It is clear, however, that the rapid and efficient dissemination of scientific results plays a major role in ensuring their combination with one another, and with earlier or later ones. On the other hand, various factors whose influence is hard to assess come into play at an early stage of consideration; the fraction of a scientist's time profitably spent perusing other people's results and methods has an upper limit which varies both with the psychology of the individual scientist and with the nature of his work. The value of secrecy and of patent protection is also a tricky problem both for governments and commercial organizations. It is fair to point out, however, that recent investigations suggest that there is certainly no overriding advantage of either type of restriction.[1]

[1] Cf. e.g. F. Machlup, *Science*, Vol. 133 (1961), p. 1463.

Another important consequence for practical policy that does allow of intelligent planning is that the combination of results from different fields (or 'cross-fertilization' as it is often called) can be drastically reduced by the existence of a very small number of fields in which there is a striking weakness. Here one must congratulate the present Minister for Science on his making a search for such 'gaps' one of his first enquiries. In this respect, one must criticize a strong tendency in the official attitude governing the support of research in this country over the last fifty years. This is that support is best given to outstanding persons rather than to outstanding fields of interest. This attitude has many points in its favour. But unless the general level of support is generous, it can easily lead, and has indeed led, to the development of gaps which are slow to become obvious and even more slowly repaired. A vicious circle develops in which for a number of years no outstanding people enter a given field, so that no financial support is given to it. After a time, the capital required to start up work in this field becomes much larger and the increased financial risk means that an even more outstanding person must come forward and ask for support if the request is to be granted. Meanwhile, however, good people fail to enter it because of the lack of inspired teaching and of financial support for research in the institutions in which they would be employed.

The effects are incalculable, but obviously bad. One gap can prevent not only the fruitful combination of results in two neighbouring fields, but can hold up work in a very wide variety of fields, and hence all their potential combinations of results as well. Again, the effects can be produced through political and economic interactions as well as through the obvious scientific ones. Past policy in this connection has tended to be: 'Always support a good man whatever field he works in. Never support anyone simply because he works in a valuable field.' I would suggest that this policy, although outstandingly successful in maintaining the peaks of scientific effort in this country, has already produced serious gaps in important fields and should be modified in the light of this experience. Once again, policy should follow the rule of maximizing the chances of success rather than minimizing the risks of being wrong, and might be phrased: 'Always support a good man whatever field he works in; always support a moderately good man unless his field is seriously overcrowded.

Be prepared to support a poor man if his field is seriously weakened. Be prepared, as a last resort, to try and deflect good men to any field in which it is becoming necessary to support poor men.'

On the whole, however, the Research Councils have carried out their difficult task admirably. Any policy threatening the independence of these Councils should be vigorously opposed by Liberals. On the other hand, while their successes are easily discerned and their errors of commission have been extremely few, one cannot be entirely satisfied with the fact that the latter have been as few as they have been: too few risks have been taken. A Liberal policy might well consider increasing the number and scope of the Research Councils and similar bodies or of keeping a watchful eye on their composition. On the whole, however, there is no justification for serious interference with the work or constitutional position of these bodies, and my own view is that Liberals should instead devote their main attention to policies bettering the condition of the universities, colleges of advanced technology, and the institutions run by the nationalized industries and services.

THE ROLE OF THE UNIVERSITIES

A vocal body of opinion has been advocating in the last year or so that the universities are forgetting that their main job is to teach. The most extreme view is that of A. P. Rowe, late Vice-Chancellor of Adelaide University, who has stated that a large part of university research is trivial and is done only for careerist reasons (cf. e.g. *If the Gown Fits* (1960)). He believes that the supposed value of combining teaching and research in the universities is quite 'mythical', and that these activities should be separated, research being carried out in research institutes preferably close to, but not necessarily within, universities. He has even suggested that the quality of teaching in provincial universities would be benefited if much university-financed research were stopped so that the money spent upon it became available for teaching purposes.

Rowe's specific criticisms have been added to by many other writers who have been taking part in a press and radio publicity campaign which is undoubtedly designed to catch the attention of the Robbins and Hale Committees, which are at present deliberating on the question of higher education in general and the universities in particular. Liberals should be in no doubt that

Rowe's specific recommendations are not only minority views but that there are very good reasons for rejecting them. They should also note that this critical press and radio campaign has been conducted by people whose qualifications are sometimes dubious and that many of their opinions show an extraordinary lack of knowledge about relatively simple aspects of university work. It is not a little strange that the one major factor underlying all the criticisms, and which is painfully obvious to all younger and many older members of universities, has been almost totally neglected in the public discussion of the last year, namely the serious financial limitations under which universities have to work.

The almost total lack of comment on this financial issue has an unpleasantly sinister aspect when one considers that for the second time running the Quinquennial Grant to the universities is under consideration at a time of serious crisis in the national economy. Liberals should be in no doubt that by and large universities in Britain are extremely poorly financed, and that unless their financial position is considerably strengthened over the next five years their ability to carry out their task efficiently will undoubtedly become seriously weakened. There is practically no idea that has been canvassed in the recent public controversy as an example of something that the universities would have adopted but for their inefficiency and conservatism, which has not in fact been seriously considered in universities for many years but dropped because it would have cost too much to put into practice.

As with primary and secondary education, successive governments have failed utterly to put their backs into the problem of finding sufficient money to give this country a really good system of higher education. The universities represent yet another example of Galbraith's 'public squalor'. What is needed is an urgent campaign to expand and improve the facilities and staffing of British universities as rapidly as possible. The most we can at present seemingly hope for is a bare maintenance of present standards.

A Liberal policy for science should aim to strengthen and encourage the universities to improve their present standards on all fronts, and should resist all tendencies to separate teaching and research in university departments. This should be done by increasing very considerably the amount of money available to them through the University Grants Committee, and by making arrange-

11

COLLEGE OF THE SEQUOIAS
LIBRARY

ments that would encourage universities to raise the salaries of all personnel and to streamline their financial methods. The removal of the customary financial stringency would itself encourage the latter tendency by removing the strongest single bar to efficient methods of expenditure. Thus it is mainly the insufficiency of available money that forces universities to use their complex multitude of controlling committees to try and see that the money is spread round the hungry mouths as fairly as possible. At present, the situation is one which no efficient business would tolerate for a moment. No realistic sums are available for works and maintenance; no money is available for capital expenditure on equipment except for newly constructed buildings; costs and plans of new buildings are inspected by a procedure which takes so long that costs are out of date by the time permission to build is granted; no subsequent modification of cost is allowed, so that extensive plans have often to be laboriously modified to bring them into line with the inflation that has occurred in prices; expansion of student intake is demanded at all costs and is the only thing that is held to justify increased staff; permission to increase staff is given too late, and insufficient allowance is made for the increased secretarial and technical staff and for the recurrent expenditure they will need.

Academics are unfortunately bad publicists on the whole, so that the true gravity of the financial position of universities in Britain today is largely unknown to the public. Most of this could easily be cured if a firm policy was laid down. Scientific departments are most strongly affected because they are in competition with industry and other countries for their staff, and because their material expenses are large. There is hardly a department in Britain today which does not owe most of its research capacity to grants from outside bodies. Rowe's suggestion that expenditure on research might be saved for teaching purposes is utterly unrealistic; the amount that could be liberated in this way is quite paltry. Rowe's view of research fails to take account of the fact that 'research', as commonly understood, fulfils two functions in a university and not just the one that is usually implied. The neglected second function of research is the *maintenance* of knowledge and techniques, as distinct from the discovery of new knowledge and techniques. This function overlaps that of postgraduate education. As at present constituted, British universities would be completely incapable of postgraduate, and in some subjects of final year honours, teaching if it were not for their research workers and the apparatus they have obtained on outside funds. It should be the aim of a Liberal policy for science to see that funds were sufficient to enable university departments to carry out their full obligations on their own, and that grants from outside funds were used for their real purpose which is the initiation of new research projects and not their long-term maintenance.

The universities are crucial to any policy for science for many reasons, but the single most compelling one is that they alone are capable of what might be called intellectual reproduction. A most important corollary for Liberals is that it is highly desirable that this vital function should be in the hands of independent institutions which have behind them the strength of traditions of independent thought and imagination.

GENERAL EFFECTS OF SCIENTIFIC ADVANCES ON HUMAN AFFAIRS

The effects of scientific research and of technological effort on human life are obvious, and they are generally recognized in fields open to public inspection. No one doubts the revolutionary effects of half a dozen new drugs on the growth of population and on the social and economic life of a large part of the world, including countries with a high standard of living. Similarly, no one doubts the profound effect upon our lives of modern methods of communication, of nuclear energy, of space-vehicles, and of the production of synthetic materials. There is some evidence and many more speculative grounds, however, upon which it is reasonable to suggest that we are little aware of the true scope and magnitude of the influence of scientific knowledge upon our lives. One can only touch very briefly upon this subject, but it represents a field of which any Liberal policy for science should take notice and at least keep under careful review. It is also a field in which the moral, ethical, and aesthetic issues cannot be separated clearly from the scientific and technical ones that are involved: political decisions cannot safely be taken on the old basis of non-scientific committees relying upon periodic advice from scientists who are not admitted to the full discussions of the whole issue. Scientists have no divine right in such issues, and will make just as many mistaken decisions as non-scientists, but if they do not play a full and equal part in the discussion of them, there is a considerable danger that the non-scientists will fail altogether to discuss them as they would have done had they been aware of the scientific developments that were relevant.

The most pressing problems likely to cause difficulty in the next ten to fifty years are in the field of biology and medicine. These fields are just reaching the degree of scientific maturity at which knowledge begins to provide previously unimaginable powers. We are already faced with the problem of the growth of population; it would have faced us sooner or later anyway, but it has been greatly accelerated by advances in chemotherapy and in the production and preservation of food. In the words of A. J. P. Taylor, these new millions are one of 'the messes' to be 'cleared up'. Work on methods of contraception is likely to provide a number of possible means of tackling the problem in the next ten years, and it will be a major exercise of scientific policy to assess their relative merits, and one in which the very best advice from biologists, doctors, sociologists, churchmen, and politicians will be needed, quite apart from the commercial interests that are bound to be involved.

This work alone is likely to result in numerous by-products which will give us the power to alter many aspects of human life which have hitherto been subject to the play of uncontrolled natural forces. Quite apart from needing to brush up our *Brave New World,* we may be faced with possibilities that were not even imagined in that fascinating novel. It is by no means inconceivable that in the next few decades it will become possible to control the sex of unborn children, to delay or advance the achievement of physical and mental maturity, to delay or advance the onset of senility, to take measures increasing the intelligence or altering the physical characteristics of young or even unborn children, and so on. These advances are unlikely to be achieved in an order which makes their application politically or socially easy. Suppose, for instance, that a method is found which raises the intelligence of male children very considerably but which fails to do so with female children. Suppose further that scientific advances have placed still greater strains upon the ability of nations to compete with one another in technological prowess and that the international situation is as tense as it is today. In the face of a strong need for men of superior intelligence, what are we going to do about it?

It is a great mistake to consider that *science* fiction is not subject to the old rule that 'truth is stranger than fiction'. In preparing to meet these possibilities, the best scientific advice is needed at all stages so that the most urgent problems receive attention first. On the other hand, social and political consequences may be pointed out by politicians and 'men of affairs' which will lead the scientists to explore technical possibilities that might otherwise not have occurred to them. One example of where we got badly out of step is on the question of 'brainwashing'. A public outcry greeted the news that began to appear in the USA shortly after the Korean war; another one followed the recent speech of a British psychiatrist which suggested that brainwashing had been used by British counter-intelligence agents during the second World War. The moral, political, and scientific questions involved have become dissociated although the scientific possibilities have been known to experimental psychologists and some psychiatrists for several decades.

Again, the technical and scientific issues attending official secrecy for security reasons are mostly beyond the reach of non-scientists at present. And yet the threat to democratic processes produced by such secrecy is potentially as great as a slip in any of the legal and economic measures which are taken by governments, and which we rightly require shall be exposed to the full range of public and parliamentary criticism before they are incorporated in our laws. To ensure a really thorough examination of such measures, we like to be sure that the political parties and government departments contain a good number of men who have been well trained in the special fields of law, business, and the armed services, and that such men are present in all spheres in which these matters are discussed and in which their eventual shape is influenced. Gradually, and only recently perceptibly, the scope of science and technology has widened so much that we can no longer treat the matter as one of simply 'taking expert advice' on appropriate occasions; science is an integral part of our civilization and culture, and democracy will only be safeguarded if the practitioners of science become an integral part of our political and economic life.

EARLY STRATEGY AND TACTICS OF A POLICY FOR SCIENCE

The nature of scientific activity has been roughly sketched above and some of the deficiencies of present policy have been outlined; it is now necessary to summarize the measures which I believe should be taken by a Liberal government to deal with the situation. First, the Minister for Science should be made a Cabinet post and a scientist appointed to the position; he should be given a permanent building for his Ministry and sufficient staff to carry out both administrative and advisory work and his own research on general scientific matters. His first task should be to find out as accurately as possible what financial measures are needed to ensure the continued health and progress of:

(*a*) university scientific departments,
(*b*) colleges of technology of all kinds,
(*c*) secondary school teaching of science and mathematics,
(*d*) the DSIR and the Research Councils, and their research institutes and units.

Following this, he should persuade the Cabinet that these fields of scientific education and research must be adequately financed and that they constitute at present the first priority in government expenditure. The first step should be to see that salaries of all types of staff in these fields are raised so that competition with industry and other countries is placed on a reasonable basis; the next, to see that their establishments are increased. These would be the first steps towards giving scientific work of all kinds an improved status in the community and thus ensuring that recruitment of first-class people was maintained or increased. This first phase should be completed rapidly and, if necessary, err on the generous side.

The next major moves would be to improve the application of science to industry, transport, and communications. Much could be done simply by instituting a much more ruthless policy towards restrictive practices and protective tariffs. Other financial inducements should also be contemplated; for instance, tax reliefs could be designed to discourage excessive expenditure on advertising and entertainment, and encourage expenditure on research and development work. The problem of the small firm unable to find the capital to start research could be met partly by offering loans to those firms willing to start research work, and partly by tax reliefs for expenditure on research contracted out to research associations or to government laboratories. The fact that some firms undoubtedly need to do less research than others is relatively unimportant; encouragement is needed in fields where significant advances can be made by scientific research, and no harm will be done by encouraging new men to enter these fields rather than the traditional soft options.

At the outset, the Minister for Science should set up a research department with a consultative branch whose main task would be to carry out operations research and to maintain a continuous survey of the actual and potential applications of scientific method to all spheres of national life. This department would start by aiming to help all governmental departments in their work; later it could offer its services on a definitely commercial basis to independent concerns of all kinds. Its activities should by no means be confined to the traditional technical fields of transport, industry, and defence, but should at the outset include sociological and economic affairs. Existing work of this kind in other Ministries should be continued, and the new department would need to be constituted in a way that prevented any of its work from conferring electoral advantages on the party in power, while providing considerable security for many of its activities.

The research department of the Ministry would also be responsible for a continual survey of scientific activity throughout the world, for long-range forecasting of future developments, and for scrutinizing the national scientific effort for weaknesses. It would also have to investigate carefully the question of international effort in science and recommend those fields in which it appeared desirable for this country to stimulate or enter into co-operative research and development.

Throughout these efforts, the Minister should carry out a long-term strategy to integrate the potentialities of scientific thought and method with other parts of our national life. An early start could be made in the educational sphere, and also by securing the appointment of scientifically trained men to the boards of nationalized industries, to government departments, and to government commissions of enquiry. Great tact and patience would be required for this part of the Minister's policy: in this, as in other parts of his work, he would be well advised to retain the goodwill, and seek frequently the advice, of existing bodies whose work has been discussed above. In all his moves, the Minister should seek to ensure the wide dissemination of scientifically trained men and women throughout those spheres in which scientific policy is shaped, for only in this way can scientific policy be democratized.

Such an expansion of scientific interest carries with it peculiar dangers of what might be called 'evil conspiracy'. It should be clearly recognized, however, that without a real policy for science, these dangers are already with us and are more likely to increase than to decrease. No Minister for Science could neglect the applications of operations research, for instance, but some of the work of his Ministry might yield information which gave great electoral advantages to the party in power. To avoid such abuses, I would suggest that the existing Advisory Council on Scientific Policy be retained and its membership expanded to include representatives of the Law, the Church, and other fields, so that its constitutional position could be modified to include that of a watching brief over the legal and political implications of scientific policy.

CONCLUSIONS

It has only been possible to scratch the surface of this immense subject, and I hope that my scientific colleagues will find pardonable the many condensations and simplifications that I have been forced to make. Despite these shortcomings, however, I hope that Liberals will accept the main burden of this essay as a spur to the urgent consideration of their attitudes upon these matters. There are many threats to liberal thought and activity facing us today which are either concerned directly with scientific policy or dependent upon it; most of them can affect seriously our economic and political health over the coming decades. It is particularly sad that the smaller issues have led to occasional bitterness and frequent hostility between scientists and non-scientists. In wartime these bitternesses held up for several years the full application of scientific method to some of the problems facing the armed services, but the stress of national danger eventually overcame them – unfortunately for this country. The present situation is one in which the dangers are less obvious and less compelling, and in which the implications are much more complicated and far-reaching than those of war. They are thus much more controversial, and the danger that current antagonisms remain unabated is much greater. For this reason, I have purposely restrained myself from the full polemical fury that some utterances of non-scientists might justifiably call forth; the position is bad enough as it is, and no good is done by throwing brickbats. On the other hand, I have not eschewed all polemic, since it is important that the opponents of science are not left in any doubt about the untenability of some of the positions they are prone to take up.

The only policy for science is indeed a Liberal one. The very nature of its progress and method is that of vigorous radicalism side by side with empirical caution; of constant flexibility co-existent with definite underlying policy. The idea that a 'policy' for this human activity could be organized from above in every detail is a contradiction in terms, as illiberal an idea as could be.

PART SIX

The World Setting

H. S. DEIGHTON

Twentieth-century Liberals are not likely to have much time for the political ideas of Thomas Hobbes. His monster state, the Leviathan, was entitled to claim all but the bare lives of its subjects in return for the hope of some physical security. It differed in some ways from modern state worship and authoritarianism, but it belonged like them to the order of things which has always, and rightly, set Liberals to sharpening their swords. The exaltation of 'reasons of state', of which Hobbes was the first great theoretician, was perhaps inevitable. It is, after all, no more than the intellectualizing, the translation on to a theoretical plane, of one of the phenomena most familiar to the student of the natural history of human societies – the instinct of every human group once formed, and whatever the purpose of its formation, to act as though its own self-preservation were the first of its duties. Without the protection of the state, wrote Hobbes, in the one of his phrases which posterity has cared to remember, 'the condition of man was nasty, brutish, and short'. It followed that he was entitled to expect, in return for his subjection to the political Leviathan, a situation in which some civilization might be evolved from savagery and, along with it, the prospect of a relative longevity.

The Liberal objection to this concept of a politics, which implies a 'trade' between ruler and ruled, is that it is bad business. It represents a sort of commerce in which the consumer is offered a good deal less than his minimum requirements. Some – all indeed who from religious or other conviction recognize an obligation transcending that of self-preservation – would hold that the price to be paid demands more of the individual than is rightly his to give. The 'movement away from honour as a principle to the fear of violent death as a principle'[1] is one which Liberals do not feel free to make. Nor do they accept that the alternative is savagery. It is of the essence of a Liberal cast of thought that the state, the political machinery of society, can and should be made progressively more appropriate to the full requirements of the individual – and that this belief confers upon the individual the obligation to assist it in so doing, as well as to

[1] Leo Strauss, *The Political Philosophy of Hobbes*, Oxford (1936), p. 129.

resist its demands when they are unreasonable. The Liberal, in fact, is neither anarchist nor authoritarian. His ruler is not an equal party in an arrangement of which the whole body of his subjects is the other. The social compact for him, to continue with this useful, if unhistorical, image, is not between some outstanding individual or class – hereinafter to be called the ruler – and the rest of the people concerned. Rather it is something arrived at in the common interest by all, something of which government is and should remain the instrument and the expression.

Hobbes's Leviathan, whatever we may think of its moral content, was a magnificent intellectual exercise. It erected a coherent theoretical structure from all the pieces of political experience which were to hand in the seventeenth century. It was a structure which had a mathematical beauty, a logicality that made it an appropriate expression of politics in the age of Descartes and Newton. But if this was the age in which the nation-state first took self-conscious form and found adequate theoretical expression, it was also, and for this reason, the age in which men became painfully aware (perhaps by contrast with the slowly growing order within their respective communities) of the existence of the international anarchy.

This situation was recognized and it was acted upon – as it had to be. Necessity and idealism had their accustomed play. Diplomacy was developed and in the treaties of Westphalia – agreements arrived at, it is worth remembering, after years of negotiation – an end was put to the Thirty Years War. Some order was achieved in the welter of separate interests which was the inevitable consequence of the Continent's divided polity. In this sphere, too, the age produced its great thinkers – but the task of Hobbes and Locke was a light one beside that of Grotius. In the Middle Ages the great canonists had sought to legislate for the whole of Christendom on the basis of Christian principles. But before the medieval order was finally at an end the greater part of thought and action in political matters had been concentrated upon the smaller and more immediately effective local spheres. The city states of medieval Italy gave rise first to the international anarchy, then to the practices of established diplomacy by which the separate units of the polity sought to maintain what could, at best, be no more than a series of viable tracks through the jungle of their relationships. The sovereign state system, the disorder of their relationship and the practice of diplomacy spread thence to envelope Europe by the seventeenth century. It has become the pattern of the world today.

Thus Hobbes's pre-Leviathan condition of disorder has survived as the context in which the separate states themselves must live. It is still the condition of all political activity. The politician, whatever his objectives, be they active or passive, radical or conservative, can only change, or preserve, a particular order of society in the first instance within his own community. If he wishes, as he may do, to influence a wider sphere he must do it through the society to which he belongs, through one unit, great or small, within the international anarchy. Whether it is socialism or profit-sharing, prohibition or race equality that he seeks, he can only hope to achieve it within a society of which these are the exterior conditions of life. He must find, make good, and sustain a sufficient clearing within the jungle in which at one remove, as it were, he still lives. If Hobbes was right – and in this at least there is no gainsaying him – to hold that the state is the instrument by which we have succeeded in rising above savagery, we must admit that the individual state has done no more than to push the savagery to its own frontiers.

This is the nature of the international scene – a disorder composed of units, whose first and overriding instinct is self-preservation. This society lives for most of the time under conditions made tolerable by the efforts of professional negotiators and of statesmen, each of whom has a duty to one unit only. The saving factor in this situation lies in the estimation held by most of the states for most of the time as to their true interests. The individual state – like the individual pre-citizen in Hobbes's nasty and brutish world, is apt, and rightly so, to regard the avoidance of a general international disorder as a major national interest. Not invariably, of course. There have been – perhaps there are – states which have sought on their own to impose their own will upon the world – their own concept of order upon the international anarchy. There have been those with less general ambitions which none the less welcome the opportunity for the pursuit of some real or seeming interest when there are troubled waters to be fished. More often than not such adventure-seeking springs from the necessity to find a solution, or a palliative, to a situation of pressing domestic crisis. *The Times,* in one of those pessimistic moods which often afflicted it during the nineteenth century, once wrote that international law could be extended no further than to 'the limit of the conscience of the strongest'. This was over-gloomy and not strictly true. For unless and until one unit of the international community possesses the power and is possessed by the will to establish a total predominance, the point at which the strongest reaches its limit is the point at which its neighbours can assemble the power and the will to stop it. The historic and recurrent counter-force for the over-mighty state (in international affairs) is the 'grand alliance'. So far the grand alliance has always emerged in response to such a situation and it has always achieved its ends. But an alliance is not a union. Its members do not, so long as they remain sovereign states, constitute a new and greater unit. Their co-operation, however close, is *ad hoc* and must be regarded as temporary. Much, perhaps all of this, will seem irrelevant to the reader who has been nurtured on the generally accepted image of the international scene in the mid-twentieth century. But the international situation has been misinterpreted and misrepresented consistently and successfully, although no perhaps with intent, since the end of the second World War. It is, of course, an arena of conflict, in which the freedom of many nations is at stake. But it was always this. It may well be that this sort of freedom is today more seriously threatened than during many long periods in the past. But if this is so, it represents a difference in degree, not one in kind. The stuff of international relations is still the relationship, perpetually changing and always the same, between sovereign states. It is not the mechanics of the struggle between those who profess and those who reject the bewilderingly mutable tenets of Marxist-Leninism.

This picture of a world absorbed in a dramatic dialectic is a Communist one – although it is the Americans who have so assiduously projected it on to the popular screen. They have done so perhaps in consequence of national character, of that predilection for one thing at a time, that preference for black and white over grey, that demand for the presentation of problems in a simple form accompanied if possible by a drastic and total solution, which is the source of so much of American strength and weakness. The unreality of this popular American – and western – assessment has been admirably stated by a practising diplomatist, who is also a distinguished historian and an American. George

Kennan complains of the tendency of his fellow-countrymen to lose sight of something which is, he says, vitally important.

This is the fact that international life normally has in it strongly competitive elements. It did not take the challenge of Communism to produce this situation. Just as there are no uncomplicated personal relationships between individuals, so, I think, there is no international relationship between sovereign states which is without its elements of antagonism, its competitive aspects. Many of the present relationships of international life are only the eroded remnants of ones which, at one time, were relationships of most uncompromising hostility. Every government is in some respects a problem for every other government, and it will always be this way so long as the sovereign state, with its supremely self-centred rationale, remains the basis of international life. The variety of historical experience and geographical situation would assure the prevalence of this situation, even if such things as human error and ambition did not.

The result is that the relationship we have with the Soviet Union has to be compared, if we are to determine its real value, not with some non-existent state of total harmony of interests, but with what we might call the normal level of recalcitrance, of sheer orneriness and unreasonableness, which we encounter in the behaviour of states anywhere, and which I am sure we often manifest in our own.[1]

International relations, in fact, are concerned, as the name implies, with the relations between nations or, more exactly, between the states in which nations find political expression. Substantial differences in values, belief, culture, and way of life, do of course profoundly and persistently influence them. Often enough these things have been the basis of national consciousness and so the source of new nation-states. If Ireland had been brought within the scope of the Common Law under Edward I, or if the Irish and the English people had emerged from the sixteenth century undivided by religion, it is reasonable to suppose that the two might now constitute a political union. More recently, the same sort of factor has produced not one but two states after the liquidation of Indian subjection. What we may loosely but conveniently call ideology has played a large part in the foundation

[1] George Kennan, *Russia and the West under Lenin and Stalin* (1961), pp. 392-3.

12

of nations and so of states. Manifestly it has much to do with their periodic attractions and repulsions, their alliances and enmities. But there seems to be no historical indication of the reverse of this picture. The view was widely held by socialists in the early years of this century that the whole concept of 'the workers' would, in a clash of fundamental loyalties, prove too strong for the established diversity of states. It vanished, in 1914, in a matter of hours. In 1917 a group of consciously and deliberately 'international' theorist-politicians acquired power in Russia, professedly as a foothold to the establishment of a new and inevitable world order. Yet within four years the group was obliged to recognize the fact that what it had accomplished was not the first stage in a world revolution, but the establishment of a new régime in one country. It had no choice but to concentrate – as its successors are still concentrating – upon the primary task of governing and strengthening Russia. After the second World War, when there were several Communist states and 'Socialism in one country' was no longer an attitude dictated by circumstance, these states continued their separate existence. For their relationship towards the original Communist government of Russia the word 'satellite' is palpably too strong, and in the case of China laughably so.

The story of Yugoslav foreign relations since the war, too, indicates that the lessons of the seventeenth century are still actively relevant. In the common view of most of Europe, the issues of the Thirty Years War lay between Protestant and Catholic. The struggle was seen as a struggle between these two ideologies. Yet the rulers of France, in what they conceived to be the national interest, intervened repeatedly and to their own advantage on the Protestant side without the least shaking the basic Catholicism of France. In the same way Yugoslavia remains, in some sort but assuredly, Communist. More recently the differing experiences and interests of China and Russia have served to give differing *national* expression to the views of the disputants in a doctrinal controversy among Marxist-Leninists. There are, in fact, a number of national states under Communist rulers. For all the attempt to present a common front and all the authority of Russia herself, it is apparent that Communist uniformity is no more a fact than western uniformity, and that the principal divisions take shape along national lines. There is no Communist monolith – if there were, no doubt, we should see a single Communist state.

The Communist danger is real enough to those who cultivate and mean to sustain a Liberal way of life. But, in allowing their passion for uncomplicated issues to lead them into publicising the image of a world dominated by the conflict between 'Communism' and its opponents, the Americans have swallowed a concept which the Communists, in their various countries, still hold to doctrinally, without invariably acting upon. From the United States itself there came consistently, throughout the crisis of 1961, most convincing evidence that this simple and dramatic view of world affairs is inadequate to the facts. It was the recurrent theme of the American argument about Berlin that if the city were to be abandoned the danger of Western Germany 'taking an eastward line' would become a very real one. This fear may be well founded, but the acceptance of it is striking evidence that international relations are still basically concerned with the relations between nations – both because the pull exerted by the sense of nationality, still more the pull of the established viable nation-state, is the most powerful of political magnets, and because whoever owes loyalty to some other political idea or cause is obliged by circumstance to give it expression through the nation-state system in which he finds himself.

Just as professional soldiers are said to concentrate upon the circumstances of the last war, so public opinion in international matters suffers under the disadvantages of a time-lag which sets a gap between the current situation and the general appreciation of it. Policy-makers must carry public opinion with them in any major issue and so this time-lag adds a good deal to the complexity of the interplay of domestic and international politics. International situations, like the public figures in Sir Harold Nicolson's book, have their public and their private faces. The one often differs much, and in ways that are important, from the other. In part this is due to the essential mutability of the international situation and to the understandable difficulty experienced by those not continuously occupied with it, in keeping pace with the changes. These difficulties are all the greater since the adjustments required are, usually at least, as much of an emotional as an intellectual exercise. Old friends become new enemies for the duration of some situation which may last for six months or for fifty years. As such, they must be resisted, not usually with force but if at all effectively, with the apparent readiness to use force as a last resort. This readiness must have a popular emotional basis. There must be not actual hatred but a powerful source of moral disapprobation, and such emotions once generated are not easily or quickly changed. Changes of this order do occur: witness the transference in the space of sixteen years of United States popular hostility from Germany and Japan to Soviet Russia and China.

The persistence of the awful confrontation of Russia and the United States of America must not be allowed to obscure the profound changes which have come over the international scene since their rivalry first made itself apparent at the time of the 1948 Berlin air-lift. For the British people, an important aspect of these changes has been a matter of their own experience. Going into the World War as a Great Power with an influence second to none, securely based upon the resources capable of justifying it, Great Britain emerged victorious in 1945. Almost a quarter of the world's populations were still more or less dependent upon Whitehall. Today, the overseas dependents of the United Kingdom are fewer than the inhabitants of the homeland, and although Britain, like France, enjoys the symbolic and at times practical attributes of a Great Power in the United Nations – a permanent seat on the Security Council and the right of veto – she does so, like France again, very much as a lesser among equals. This is not to say that there is no substance in the tributes – so often paid on public occasions by American leaders – to her special influence and to the particular merit which her diplomacy and statesmanship may derive from her long experience in world affairs. For historical reasons the influence of Britain is still remarkably widespread. A good many of the most diverse powers are still willing to seek British advice, to heed British warnings, or to glance at British examples in matters of politics and administration – although this too is palpably becoming slowly less so. Despite the lessening of her relative weight in political affairs, Britain can still call upon a standard of diplomatic practice which is second to none. But there are less agreeable corollaries of this state of affairs, in the shape of a world-wide burden of commitments arising from a real sense of responsibility and an ill-founded pursuit of influence and status. These have been shown to be too great for her to bear without inefficiency and without a serious drain upon her resources.

The decline of British power, along with the ending of the British empire and the transformation of the Commonwealth into a special relationship of uncertain significance, is only one among the number of major changes of the past decade and a half. China, upon whose treatment as a Great Power President Roosevelt had insisted during the second World War in spite of British doubts, is now plainly entitled to that status – which indeed British statecraft has long been prepared to accord her. But it is no longer a China upon which the United States would be prepared to lavish patronage. And the emergence of a Communist China in open dispute with the Soviet Union has made plain the unreality of that interpretation of world affairs as a straightforward confrontation of two blocks of the 'free' and the Communist and which regards the latter as unbreakably monolithic.

An alliance is a notoriously fragile arrangement. Only those alliances which neither party takes very seriously, and which in consequence neither is likely to subject to a serious test, survive very long. The ancient Anglo-Portuguese alliance and the wartime Anglo-Soviet alliance are cases in point. An effective alliance is, in fact, no more than the practical expression given by two or more powers to a sense of immediate high common interest. It usually survives as an effective instrument just so long as each ally is prepared to give to that interest a sufficiently high priority in its scheme of things.

Towards the end of the year 1856, Palmerston, then Prime Minister, learned that his Foreign Secretary was growing alarmed at the swift erosion of the unity of purpose which had held the governments of Britain and France together during the Crimean War. 'This', he wrote,

> is of the nature of things and should have been expected sooner or later . . . during the war all the separate interests and feelings of the two governments and countries were forgotten in the common exertions for a common and paramount object. That object attained, the separate interests and feelings again come into play. Just as the stars become visible when the moon ceases to shine . . . intimate alliance cannot long subsist between equal powers. Those relations can be lasting only between a stronger and a weaker state.[1]

This lesson, which sprang from Palmerston's already long experi-

---

[1] Bodleian Library (Clarendon Deposit).

ence of the relationship of sovereign states, might as readily be applied to the consideration of the stories of the two major power blocks in the past fifteen years. Continental Western Europe lay for a while after the end of the war, with its economy in ruins, militarily at the mercy of the Soviet Union. The Red divisions stood, in the language of the accepted military advisers of the time, 'four days from the Channel'. In this situation the Americans still immune, even remote, themselves, acted with promptitude and remarkable statesmanship. The Marshall Plan offered Europe the means for its economic revival. The North Atlantic Treaty Organization wove the majority of the threatened powers, together with the United States and Canada, into an alliance which the strength of the United States then made unchallengeable. Under this shield the economic revival, touched off – and made possible – by the Marshall Plan, achieved a resounding success. By 1961 Europe's economic dependence upon the United States was a thing of the past. That much was apparent from the proceedings of the International Monetary Fund meeting at Vienna in the early autumn of that year. For the first time it was not the United States but the great trading countries of continental Europe which dominated the scene and called the tune. The economic renaissance of Europe had gone so far that, for the first time, it was not the United States dollar but the French franc, the lira and the Deutschmark which were in demand.

American observers at the time seemed to regard this manifestation of strength and independence on the part of their former protégés as significant of no more than a temporary challenge to their economic predominance. But the reality of European economic strength is incontrovertible. Although the Common Market area has a slightly smaller population than the United States, it would be more populous than either the United States or Russia if Britain were to join it. It has a well-established pattern of economic growth and a pattern of lower costs and lower living standards which might be expected to sustain the growth and offset in some degree the rather greater wealth of North America in raw materials. In any case the extent to which raw materials and tropical products are readily available to the Common Market countries will depend upon the arrangements which are eventually made with the Commonwealth and other associated overseas territories. It is important not to lose sight of the extent to which this achievement and the prospects which it holds out are the result of a conscious and continuing determination to free Europe from the predominance of that American economy, to the generous and farsighted use of which the European recovery initially owed so much. It is right to assume that by 1970 – and in all likelihood some time before that date – the West will have not one but two major economic powers, with Europe quite predominant within its own area and increasingly near to parity of influence with the United States in the rest of the non-communist world.

The significant thing about the sense of competition with the United States, which pervades the directorate of Europe's advancing economy, is that it is a measure of the almost unrelieved failure of the Russians and their client states in Eastern Europe to present Western Europe with a challenge which, military considerations apart, they need take at all seriously. Ulbricht's famous, or infamous, Berlin wall was an outright confession of the economic and political failure of the Russian system in Eastern Europe. Any substance there might be in Mr Krushchev's claim that Russian production and living standards will overhaul those of the United States within a measurable distance of time has certainly escaped the notice of those who are the nearest neighbours of the Soviet Union's most advanced dependents. In Europe, Russian and, in part for that reason, American influence is palpably on the defensive. Russia has become once again what she was in the decades before the Crimean War, the great force of continental conservatism, of resistance to change. History may well come to show, although it will take a long time to do so, that the motive force behind the Russian pressure for settlement in Berlin has been the awareness that in five or ten years' time they would have to deal in this, as in all other purely European matters, not, as now, primarily with the United States but with Europe itself.

It is true that in some major European countries the Communist party has still a following. But, while the party machines remain, and are likely to remain, powerful, professional, and potentially dangerous to internal security, it is difficult to believe that the number of their card-holding supporters, and still more of those who support them with their votes, is significant of much more than the efficiency and ruthlessness of their organization and their attraction for that large number of the electorate[1] who are by tradition – even by heredity – wedded to the concept of radical opposition and violent change. These however are the attitudes of those who count themselves as the 'have-nots' of European society. The arrogance of power or the flaunting of wealth in 'conspicuous expenditure' still turn men's minds to Communism as a handy stone that might be thrown. But there are now few Europeans, outside the blinkered and the committed professionals, who are prepared to regard what Russia has to offer as a serious, viable, and potentially acceptable way of life. Europe (if we may employ, as a matter of convenience, so vast a generalization) is no longer afraid of the ideology of her eastern neighbours. Fear of Russian military power is of course another thing. But here again the situation has changed almost beyond recognition since the beginning of the Cold War.

No one can say how far there was a real likelihood of Russian aggression in Western Europe at the time of the Berlin air-lift. But the possibility was adjudged sufficiently real to bring back United States bombers to British airfields – and with atomic weapons. This measure, entirely precautionary though it was, has a certain historical interest as the one gesture of total military supremacy that the world has ever seen. The prohibition which it imposed on a further Russian advance into Europe was absolute. The Soviet had no defence against the destruction which the nuclear monopoly could bring to them – and nowhere in the world any prospect of military assistance capable of offsetting this disadvantage. Two years later came the explosion of the first Russian atomic device, and, with the growth of the Russian nuclear stockpile and the modernization of the Russian air force, there arose the now familiar two-power world. Whether the Soviet Union has ever contemplated the advance of its aims by military means is and must remain a moot question. Mr Kennan apparently holds that it has not done so and that it is not an integral part of Marxist-Leninism to advance the cause of a Communist state by military means. If we accept this we must exclude the example of the Russian attack upon Finland, when perhaps the Russians expected as little resistance as they had met with in Poland. Whatever the truth of this assumption – and in

[1] In France it has been credibly estimated at an average of 25% since the Revolution.

orthodox Communist theory successful war against a capitalist power could achieve no more than the speeding up of the inevitable – it is one which no government would be justified in making.

After the initial return to Europe, American policy sought – and successfully – to establish the sense of security by the characteristic encouragement of self-help. As with economic affairs through the Marshall Plan, so now through the establishment of NATO, the United States reconstructed the defences of Europe. But the principal protection came still through the guarantee of American involvement which was built into the treaty that called the Organization into being. Given the adherence to it of the United States, the essential practical aspect of that agreement was the provision that an attack made upon any one member of the organization should be treated as an attack upon all. The United States provided an effective shield for Western Europe in the shape of the undertaking to make a massive and, no doubt, crushing retaliation if Europe were attacked.

This doctrine of 'massive retaliation' had as its instrument the resources of the Strategic Air Command, based largely upon airfields outside, and far from, the continental United States. It gave effect to the policy enunciated in the NATO treaty, which has been adequately expressed in the words 'you touch one of my friends and I will blow you to pieces'. The doctrine was enunciated at the time when the American homeland was itself virtually free from all fear of direct involvement in a nuclear war. The disappearance of that American immunity is the cardinal difference between the world military situation ten years ago and that of the 1960s. The capacity of the United States to destroy Russia is no doubt greater today than ever it was, but it exists now in the context of a comparable, if not an equal, capacity in the Soviet Union to destroy the United States. An ever-increasing interest on both sides is now directed to the development and production of the so-called 'second-strike' weapons of which the Polaris armed, long-endurance, submarine is the most conspicuous example. The purpose of these weapons is to make possible the destruction of an enemy's homeland even though the United States itself should fall victim to a major nuclear disaster.

A few years ago the United States could, and did, seek to deter an attack upon her allies by mounting and maintaining a threat

13

of overwhelming punishment. Now she seeks to deter an attack upon herself by guaranteeing vengeance. Similar changes, although of course on a smaller scale, have taken place in strategic thinking and planning in the United Kingdom. The Defence White Paper of 1957 embodied the threat that if Russia attacked in Europe with *any* forces, nuclear or not, nuclear weapons carried by the Blue Streak rocket would destroy the Soviet Union. But this retaliatory doctrine has had to be abandoned. Blue Streak was 'soft' and the policy suicidal – so now Britain too has moved on to the building up of what may be termed 'vengeance-capacity'.

Whether or not there has been at any time a real danger of physical aggression from the east, no one can positively say. But the possibility of it without the existence of a deterrent system is not in question. Nor is the justice of the assumption that, necessary or not, such a system does have the capacity to deter. The great question for Europe is whether the existing shield of deterrent can be indefinitely depended upon. The indications are that it cannot. It must be thought at least unlikely that the American government will continue to see it as its duty to bring the continental United States under a direct danger of incineration by reacting with nuclear weapons to an aggression against some part of Western Europe.

This sort of situation, for which it would be unjust to blame the United States government, whose overriding duty is to its own people, has long been foreseen. It was this, rather than any hankering for the supposed symbols of a Great Power which was the justification as well, no doubt, as the principal motive for the creation of British nuclear capacity. Similar considerations have long been at work in France and it is German anxieties arising from the same process of thought which are today the most important dissolvent force in the NATO alliance. Ever since it became apparent that Russia possessed, in significant quantity, the means to strike the continental United States, the American government has, and rightly, grown increasingly concerned to limit and control the power of setting off any kind of nuclear war. American defence theorists have talked in ever-widening terms of a 'nuclear threshold', in effect the imposition of a pause for reflection upon an aggressor who uses conventional weapons. NATO thinking has for some time assumed the use of 'tactical' nuclear weapons to bring to a halt an otherwise overwhelming attack by conventional forces. But the United States is now palpably, and understandably, in retreat from such thinking. Dr Kissinger, most prominent of the American theoreticians of the limited nuclear war, has now announced his conversion to the doctrines of a dependence upon conventional weapons until the last possible moment. The argument seems to be that nuclear war, at any rate, is indivisible. In the context of the fact that it is also unthinkable, that doctrine need not be looked upon as one of despair.

The dilemma of the atomic powers of today arises from the classic weakness of an alliance between sovereign states. The next stage is the first in political unification, a process which cannot but have its upshot in the comprehension of the allies in some new sovereignty – federation, confederation or unified state. Political sovereignty – a state – is in fact, as Hobbes in his own way made clear, the expression of a more or less permanent community of interests. The problems of Western Europe, in the present age of deterrence by threat of vengeance, seem plainly to point in the direction of some such political expression of the emergent European consciousness.

The desire for a locally controlled nuclear deterrent – principally a German desire at present – seems likely of itself to lead, within a decade at most, to some sort of military arrangement which will mean the effective surrender of sovereignty, especially of the sole control of foreign and military policy, by the member-states of Western Europe. But there are other and scarcely less compelling reasons why we may expect to see the ever-growing political expression of Europe. Economic integration and interdependence, when pursued to the extent envisaded by the Treaty of Rome, could not fail to bring corresponding developments in the political sphere. In fact, the ideas of those who created and of the majority of those who still lead the European Economic Community have always been concerned with the creation of some sort of political union. A common European consciousness – indefinable but unmistakable – affords, it is scarcely too much to say, little less emotional basis for eventual nationhood than existed between the thirteen colonies of the eastern seaboard of North America in the years before the formation of the Union.

Historically, one of the most potent forces in the creation of that common awareness of nationality upon which all effective and permanent political groups are dependent is the pressure and competition of external, and differing, views and interests. It was the belief of Americans in the existence of a community of interests as against Great Britain, transcending the many differences between them, which brought about the – at the time seemingly unlikely – American union. Unwillingness to accept a continuing secondary role and the knowledge that only union can make a primary one possible, has been a moving force in the emergence of Europe. All things considered, the period of Europe's dependence upon the United States has passed with surprisingly little serious friction, especially in strictly European matters. The familiar slogan 'Yank go home' has been much too obviously expressive of really sinister and far from genuinely European interests to be significant of any sentiment beyond an irritation of a predictable kind. Indeed, so far from the presence of substantial United States forces on the Continent having been the irritant which brought Europe together, it may be said to have afforded the sense of security without which the more serious divisions could scarcely have been healed. Without the presence of American (and to a lesser extent British) garrisons on the Continent the most fundamental of Europe's divisive forces, the French fear of Germany, could hardly have been bridged to anything like the extent we now see. But outside the Continent the picture is a different one. In Asia and Africa, as the tide of direct European influence ebbed, the United States of America was confronted with a vast battleground of conflicting ideologies and aspirants to power. Despite her record in Latin America, and with lapses in which independent corporations and individuals rather than government agencies were responsible, she has pursued policies broadly in accordance with the public image which it has been the object of Americans to sustain since the Declaration of Independence and the writing of the Constitution. It may be that her policies have in general been the right ones. From a Liberal point of view this seems very likely true. But there have been frequent and increasing conflicts between American policies and various European interests which have begun to create a common European sentiment against the United States in this field.

The issues involved are by no means peripheral to the basic politics of some of the European states concerned. In France in the 1950s the problem of Algeria was basic – the determinant of political direction. In Belgium, African affairs are only less of a political and economic factor, and even in Britain, politics have, at times, seemed to turn upon the reading of the signs in Central Africa. The extent to which Italian affairs have been influenced by relations with the Arab countries and the activities in them of Signor Enrico Mattei is often overlooked. In France, and to a lesser extent in Italy, there are discernible connections between domestic politics and the Arab-Israeli imbroglio. European affairs are necesarily, as ever, closely concerned with both sides of the Mediterranean Sea and this alone, since the states of the southern littoral are deeply involved in the politics of black Africa, means that Europe is scarcely less concerned with the development of affairs in Africa than when most of that continent was directly ruled from Europe. A common policy in Africa and in the Middle East is a pressing need of Europe and may be expected to be one of the earliest political manifestations of the concentration of sovereignties which is the direction – and the conscious and deliberate direction – of the European movement.

What we are now witnessing in Western Europe, and what we are now obliged to make a series of fundamental decisions upon, is something much more than a major economic adjustment, although it is certainly that. It is also, and even more essentially, a political development – the creation of a new and, by any standard, gigantic supra-state, and by a process which cannot fail to involve the integration and consequent loss of individual national sovereignties in the greater. This has come about within NATO and, so far, under the shield of American power. The circumstances which gave rise to that alliance are still in substantial existence. The need is still there, but just because a mere alliance is an *ad hoc* device, the very persistence of the need for it makes alliance alone an inadequate piece of machinery. Enduring alliances, as Palmerston knew, only survive on a basis of inequality as between the allies. It is this inequality, as against the United States, which Europe is plainly rejecting. But, by the same token, the existing alliance alone will provide no permanent solution of Europe's differences with Russia, and in a totally different degree with the United States. The era when the West consisted, politically and militarily, of the United States surrounded by a cluster of dependent allies is approaching its end. It is inacceptable to the European states, and, no less, it is no longer acceptable to the

United States themselves. Senator Fulbright[1] has said that it would be 'tragic folly' to assume that the Commonwealth can rely for its security solely upon the United States which had neither the resources nor the will to provide alone for the security of the free world. And he gave one reason, in itself sufficient if true, for Britain's adhesion to a European union, when he acknowledged that the spectacle of German military resurgence was properly disturbing and indeed provocative to Russia, and added the belief that without British adhesion to it Western Germany would dominate the European community.

Just because of what it would inevitably entail, a nuclear war seems unlikely. Aside from the possible lunatic, those who possess the 'deterrent' are likely to be themselves deterred. This danger may be equated except for scale with that which every motorist every day faces when he passes an oncoming driver at speed. The danger will of course become more real as the possession of nuclear military capacity becomes more widespread, as, if unchecked, it is likely to do. And herein perhaps lies the best chance of a first, irrevocable, step towards world government. The common interests of the nuclear power in limiting, even in prohibiting, the increase in their number is still so overwhelmingly the most potent of all interests in common between states that the prospect of its eventually bringing them into collaboration with this end in view can never be absent. The possibility of a *Pax Uranica*[2] is still with us, and it carries with it the possibility of world government.

In the meantime, while Africa proliferates new sovereign states, while the Communist world loses even the appearance of monolithic unity, and while Arab unity remains a sentiment, the Hobbesian jungle of European international relations seems certain to yield to some sort of Leviathan. Within ten years at most it appears reasonable to assume that the western alliance will contain not one but two powers of the first magnitude. The United States of America will have been joined by the equivalent of a United States of Europe.

The public demonstration of the diminution of British power was invited – and received – when the Eden Government

---

[1] In his speech to the Commonwealth Parliamentary Association in London and in his article in *Foreign Affairs* (1962).
[2] See my chapter in the *Unservile State* (1957), pp. 271–2.

embarked upon the Suez aberration. The realization of Britain's new position, its consequences, and the changes of policy for which it called, came in 1961. Then those forces became apparent which were driving Britain into the Common Market – and the Conservative party accepted them, although its leaders discreetly veiled the wide political implications of the process, inescapable as they are. Thus we stand at the beginning of a new stage in our history. It will be one in which our influence in world affairs, although it cannot but be considerable and could well be decisive, will be less and less direct and more and more exercised through our membership of the European community and in co-operation with our European partners. The issue whether or not to 'join Europe' is no longer a real one, for an alternative does not exist. Economically an attempt to 'go it alone' might reduce us to a dependence upon barter.[1] Politically a policy of independence would in effect mean a degree of dependence upon the United States which would be acceptable neither to us nor to the Americans. The corollary of Europe's growing self-reliance and independence of the United States has been American encouragement of that process from motives of which a genuine liberalism, and an understandable desire for a partner strong enough to share the bearing of the free world's burdens, form the greater part.

Whether we like it or not, our immediate fortune lies with Europe – and the issues which will dominate us during the next ten or twenty years are likely to be European ones. Our principal problem is to fit ourselves into Europe. The interests and personalities of Paris, Bonn, Rome, The Hague, and Brussels will be our most intimate concerns. The affairs of Europe will matter more to us than at any time of peace since the eighteenth century.

We shall be in the position of belonging to the European community and also to the Commonwealth community. But to the one we shall be bound by a businesslike nexus of treaties and by the surrender of sovereignty. To the other we shall be tied by something less concrete. This does not mean that we are, politically, to sacrifice the Commonwealth for Europe, as is still sometimes suggested. What we ought perhaps to sacrifice is the illusion of which this attitude is significant. For it *is* an illusion to suppose that the continuance of the Commonwealth connection has, in

[1] As Sir Oliver Franks suggested in his valedictory speech as Chairman of Lloyds Bank.

some mysterious way, compensated for the loss of the Empire which it replaced and allowed us thereby to remain within striking distance, power-wise, of international giant status. Domestically, it may well be that we have cause to be thankful for this impression. Without the inspiration and satisfaction which has fairly been derived from the spectacle of a once-dependent Empire evolving into a free Commonwealth, the disappearance of the old imperial image could hardly have taken place without serious repercussions at home. The 'Empire Loyalists' might have been lifted, not indeed out of idiocy, but into some sort of temporary significance. In the wider field the Commonwealth has long ceased to be an instrument for projecting and magnifying the image and influence of the United Kingdom. Our sister states within the Commonwealth are no longer daughter states – still less are they British auxiliaries with votes at UNO. When our responsibility for each was ended we not only gave them a latch-key – we handed over the freehold. Much sentiment remained – made amply and grandly manifest in many thousands of war graves. Much remains too – qualified but real, common citizenship, open diplomatic exchanges, a permeating complex of consultative organs, a great mass of professional contacts – even a regular Commonwealth Conference of lecturers in French. This is something which it is difficult to quantify but is immensely worthwhile. But it is not political power, it is not political union – it is not even an alliance. And – it is not merely British. It is important to get our thinking about the Commonwealth into the right perspective – we might start with the thought that it could very well go on without us.

For Liberals there is every reason to welcome the emergence of Europe and the prospect of Britain's absorption into it. Nor need they feel that the ideals of a liberal-empire from which the concept of the Commonwealth sprang will necessarily be for ever lost in the corridors of time. The liberal-empire and the Commonwealth were the reaction of liberal thought and influence to a world order in which Great Britain was obliged to acquire influence and authority in many places overseas. Now they will be obliged in the same way to use all the influence they can command in Britain's new sphere. It must be their first purpose in foreign policy to see to it, so far as they are able, that the shape and policies of the new community develop along the lines of freedom and the rule of law and that the social and economic measures it adopts are directed towards liberal objectives by policies arrived at pragmatically in the light of a continuing and radical examination of the facts. Once Britain becomes a part of Europe it will be a principal, and it may be presumed increasingly a domestic, task for Liberals to pursue the achievement and maintenance of a liberal Europe – and of such a Europe to strengthen its ties with like-minded societies overseas.

It has become a commonplace that entry into the Common Market, while it will immensely increase the opportunities, will also exacerbate the difficulties of the British economy by exposing its weaknesses to the cold winds of commerce. Something of the same kind must also be expected to happen to British politics. There is upon the continent of Europe much with which Liberals will find themselves in sympathy, but there is also plenty of illiberalism. In some places, positively illiberal forces are a good deal more powerful than they have been for a long time here. There are strong Communist parties in France and Italy, and in France and elsewhere the contrary kind of authoritarian sentiment is far from negligible. Political freedom, in its more elemental forms of the freedom of expression and the protection afforded by the rule of law, has been pretty much assured in Britain for a long time. The radical, the critic, even the eccentric, has long had an easier time than he enjoys, even today, in several parts of Europe and in any part of the United States. A growing unity among the nations of Western Europe cannot but mean that many things which, while absolute sovereignty prevails, are regarded as domestic will become the concern of all of the partners. In this sense it seems fair to say that British Liberals, like British industry, have been enjoying a sheltered existence. It will obviously be a principal aim of Liberals, whether in opposition or in power, to build and maintain the sort of European community in which the fundamentals of freedom are generally expected and extended. But it is too much to hope that the relatively quiet life of British politics will not be exposed to more vigorous, and invigorating, forces. All this is not necessarily so much loss. Liberal Britons will find battle-hardened veterans among their comrades in the new community. There are plenty of Germans whose belief in liberal values has led them through the barbed wire which surrounded the concentration camps and has survived under the shadow of the incinerator chimneys. A great number of French men and women are at this present time positively staking their security, and even their lives, upon their belief in freedom. It is a long time since an Englishman, in his own country, was called upon to make so positively dangerous a stand for his political beliefs as that made by Miss Bardot when she declined to pay tribute to the Organization of the Secret Army.

It is at present in France that these illiberal forces are principally and most dangerously active. That they are so is principally, almost entirely indeed, a consequence of those world-wide developments of which the changing and diminishing connections between Great Britain and the Commonwealth are themselves a part. There seems no reason to suppose that the restoration of Europe, which would take the first place in British considerations, will necessarily do anything to hasten the process by which the Commonwealth ties have been, and are being, altered. The principal difference in the Commonwealth relationship seems likely to be that it will become a part of the wider and highly important relationship between the whole of Western Europe and the sum of those many areas overseas in which there are still European interests and an active European influence. There seems very little reason why anyone should lose by this. It is too often forgotten that the sad story of the end of the French empire, beginning in south-east Asia and Madagascar and ending in tragedy in Algeria, is less than a half of that story. On the principle perhaps that only bad news is news, the parallel history of France in black Africa has been given little attention even in France itself. The French achievement may well turn out to have been more effective and more durable than our own. It is very far from being one of unrelieved failure. There is good reason to hope. But a European community which contains both the British and the French will have a more enduring influence upon the future of Africa than either the British or the French could ever have alone, still more so when their governments are formulating and pursuing common policies with the non-colonial influences of the rich and eager investors of Western Germany. A united and growing political union on the Continent does not mean an end of the activity and influence of Europe in the under-developed territories of the world. It could mean a stronger and more co-ordinated one. The anger of some Belgians, the defiance of the

European mercenaries in Katanga, and the desperate anarchy created by the *colons* or by those many French officers who are tortured by the picture of the betrayal of the Moslems to whom they promised protection in Algeria, must not be allowed to obscure the fact that Europe's role in Africa and Asia can by no means be summed up in the two words 'settlers' and 'Salazar'. A reasonably liberal Europe, such as we are entitled to hope for, can do much to co-ordinate, share in, and modify, along with the United States, the policy of the great free powers in the under-developed world.

Nor, of course, is adherence to the concept and the growing fact of a united Europe in any sense a withdrawal from that of the United Nations. The United Nations Organization, even if it were nothing else, would command our support merely because it expresses the plain fact that the world should increasingly be thought of as one, and because its principles do enshrine some of the essentials of a decent world order. It is of course much more, and of much more immediate practical value than that. Its achievements are less spectacular than its failures, but in fields like health, education, and the care of refugees they have been, and continue to be, great. From the point of view of the ultimate ideal, and necessity, of world government, its weakness is plain. It is composed of member states who are not yet ready for world government. To say this is not simply to say that the member states of the United Nations Organization are merely, and selfishly, clinging to their several sovereignties. No doubt they are, and will continue for a good many years to do so. But there is more to it than that. The real issue is the kind of society which will exist under that order to which sovereignty is to be surrendered. Sovereignty in itself is certainly nothing to be particularly proud of, nothing to be cherished and defended at all times and at all costs. Such slogans as 'my country right or wrong' are the manifestations of despair and of an unhappy conscience. What Liberals need, and have always sought, is membership of a community in which their political consciences may be reasonably at ease. So far they have had to seek this within the boundaries of an already existing nation-state. Thus it has been that the free society of Locke and Gladstone came into being within the framework provided, in the first place, by Hobbes's Leviathan. Most often, in the recent past, an urgent desire for national freedom has expressed itself in the division of existing states and empires. But this is not inevitable. The thirteen colonies, once free, sought to preserve their freedom and their livelihoods in a greater union made possible by the prevailing preponderance of the things they had in common. Something of the same order is happening in Europe today, and there is no reason why it should be confined to Europe. There is nothing fanciful in the suggestion that the economic and political problems which Britain's adhesion to the Common Market would create for New Zealand might be solved by her joining the United Kingdom, if she wished, as Malta was once invited to do, in some such way as Northern Ireland is a part of it. It seems unlikely that the New Zealanders would wish to blur their identity in this way – but the possibility remains. The unity of Europe is a great undertaking, its pursuit is likely to be long and absorbing – yet it is surely right to think of it as part of a still wider process. Ireland herself after struggling free of a forced union with Britain will see nothing but advantage in membership along with the United Kingdom in a greater, European whole. The way out of the Hobbesian jungle lies through the clearance and settlement of isolated patches and then through the union of those which seek to order their affairs alike.

Notes on Contributors

R. B. MC CALLUM, Master of Pembroke College, Oxford, is the chairman of the Oxford Liberal Group. He is the author of *The Life of Asquith* (1936) and *Public Opinion and the Last Peace* (1944). He completed the fourth volume of Halévy's *History of the English People in the Nineteenth Century* (1951) and was the originator of the Nuffield College series of General Election studies, and co-author of *The British General Election of 1945* (1947).

MARK BONHAM CARTER is a member of the Organizing Committee of the Liberal Party. He studied at Balliol College, Oxford and later went to Chicago University as Commonwealth Fellow. He was M.P. for Torrington from 1958 to 1959, is a director of the Royal Opera House, and is a publisher by profession.

PETER WILES is a professor of economics at Brandeis University. He is a former Fellow of All Souls College and of New College, Oxford, co-author of *The Unservile State* (1957), and author of *Price, Cost, and Output* (1958) and *The Political Economy of Communism* (1962).

WALTER ELTIS is an economist, and a Lecturer at Exeter College, Oxford.

A. D. C. PETERSON is director of the Department of Education of Oxford University and chairman of the Liberal Education Association. He was deputy director of Psychological Warfare in South-east Asia (1944–6), headmaster of Adams' Grammar School (1946–52) and of Dover College (1954–7), and director-general of Information in Malaya (1952–4). He is the author of *The Far East* (1948), *100 Years of Education* (1952), and *Educating our Rulers* (1957).

IAN E. BUSH is professor of physiology at Birmingham University and author of *Chromatography of Steroids* (1961).

H. S. DEIGHTON is an historian, and a Fellow of Pembroke College, Oxford. He was chairman of the Middle East Group of Chatham House (1943–6) and co-author of *The Unservile State* (1957).

Index

COLLEGE OF THE SEQUOIAS
LIBRARY